D0102484

Betty Crocker

soups &
stews

100 Recipes for the Way You Really Cook

WILEY

Wiley Publishing, Inc

Copyright © 2009 by General Mills, Minneapolis, Minnesota. All rights reserved.

Published by Wiley Publishing, Inc., Hoboken, New Jersey

Published simultaneously in Canada

For general information on our other products and services or for technical support, please contact our Customer Care Department within the United States at (800) 762-2974, outside the United States at (317) 572-3993 or fax (317) 572-4002.

Wiley also publishes its books in a variety of electronic formats. Some content that appears in print may not be available in electronic books. For more information about Wiley products, visit our web site at www.wiley.com.

Library of Congress Cataloging-in-Publication Data:
Crocker, Betty.
  Betty Crocker soups and stews : 100 recipes for the way you really cook.
      p. cm.
  Includes index.
  ISBN 978-0-470-39796-1 (cloth : alk. paper)
  1. Soups. 2. Stews. I. Title. II. Title: Soups and stews.
  TX757.C74 2009
  641.8'13—dc22

                                    2008026380

General Mills

Editorial Director:
Jeff Nowak

Manager and Editor:
Lois Tlusty

Recipe Development and Testing:
Betty Crocker Kitchens

Photography: General Mills Photography
Studios and Image Library

Wiley Publishing, Inc.

Publisher: Natalie Chapman

Executive Editor: Anne Ficklen

Editor: Adam Kowit

Production Editor: David Sassian

Cover Design: Suzanne Sunwoo

Interior Design: Tai Blanche

Layout: Indianapolis Composition Services

Manufacturing Manager: Kevin Watt

Printed in China

10 9 8 7 6 5 4 3 2 1

Our Betty Crocker Kitchens seal guarantees success in your kitchen. Every recipe has been tested in America's Most Trusted Kitchens™ to meet our high standards of reliability, easy preparation and great taste.

Cover photo: Beef and Potato Stew (page 146)   Find more great ideas at **BettyCrocker.com**

Dear Friends,

Isn't it amazing that something as simple as soup can hold so many possibilities? The variety of ingredients, methods of preparation, flavors of the season and your mood and your schedule—all these make for endless delicious combinations.

You could cozy up to the comfort of a steaming bowl of classic Chicken Noodle or Chunky Tomato Soup. Or spice up your day with Chipotle Pork Chili. Satisfy the hungriest of hungries with slow cooker Beef and Potato Stew and get a fresh veggie fix with Ratatouille Soup.

Whatever your family's favorites are, there's a soup, stew, chili or chowder to fit the bill—hot or cold, quick or slowly simmered and as a starter or a whole dinner in a bowl.

So get out the bowls and spoons and tell the family, "Soup's on!"

Enjoy,

Betty Crocker

contents

Great Garnishes

To make your soup or stew look and taste even more delicious, try topping with one of the following garnishes.

TOP WITH VEGGIES

Chopped avocado

Chopped bell pepper

Chopped broccoli

Chopped tomato

Chopped cucumber

Chopped green onion

Sliced mushrooms

NUTS OR SEEDS

Cashews

Pine nuts

Popcorn

Sliced or slivered almonds

Sunflower nuts

Toasted sesame seed

FRUIT

Sliced apple

Sliced mango

Sliced pear

SOMETHING SALTY

Crumbled cooked bacon

Crumbled feta or blue cheese

Crushed corn or tortilla chips

Pretzels

Shredded cheese

SWIRL IN OR DOLLOP WITH

Guacamole

Pesto

Salsa

Sour cream or yogurt

ARRANGE ON TOP

Bagel chips

Bell pepper cutouts

Chopped crystallized ginger

Edible flowers (pansies, nasturtiums, citrus blossoms, marigolds, petunias)

Fresh herbs (parsley, dill weed, fennel, cilantro, rosemary)

Lemon or lime peel strips

Lime wedges or slices

Piped mashed potatoes

Tiny or small shrimp, cooked

Soup Storage Success

Soups, stews and chilies are ideal make-ahead dishes. Here's how to keep them fresh and ready to reheat in time for lunch or dinner.

Refrigerate most soups, stews and chilies up to three days. Refrigerate those made with fish and shellfish for one day.

To freeze soup, stew or chili, pour into resealable plastic containers, leaving ¼ to ½ inch headspace because it will expand as it freezes. Stored this way, they will keep up to three months.

To reheat your broth-based soup, place over medium heat, stirring occasionally, until hot; or reheat in the microwave.

Heat thick purees or soups containing milk, cream, eggs or cheese over low heat, stirring frequently. Don't let them boil or the ingredients may separate.

Freezing soup sometimes changes its flavor, so you may need to adjust the seasonings to taste during reheating.

Four Basic Broths

Keep broths on hand to make homemade soups and stews anytime.

Beef and Broth

Prep Time: 30 min
Start to Finish: 3 hr 45 min
About 6 cups broth and 1 cup cooked beef

2 lb beef shank crosscuts or soup bones
6 cups cold water
1 teaspoon salt
¼ teaspoon dried thyme leaves
1 medium carrot, cut up
1 medium stalk celery with leaves, cut up
1 small onion, cut up
5 peppercorns
3 whole cloves
3 sprigs parsley
1 bay leaf

1. Remove marrow from centers of bones. In 4-quart Dutch oven, melt marrow over low heat, or heat 2 tablespoons vegetable oil until hot. Cook beef shanks in marrow over medium heat until brown on both sides.

2. Add water; heat to boiling. Skim foam from broth. Stir in remaining ingredients; heat to boiling. Skim foam from broth; reduce heat. Cover and simmer 3 hours.

3. Remove beef from broth. Cool beef about 10 minutes or just until cool enough to handle. Strain broth through cheesecloth-lined sieve; discard vegetables and seasonings.

4. Remove beef from bones. Cut beef into ½-inch pieces. Skim fat from broth. Use broth and beef immediately, or cover and refrigerate broth and beef in separate containers up to 24 hours or freeze up to 6 months.

Slow Cooker Directions: Decrease water to 5 cups. Increase salt to 1¼ teaspoons. Heat 2 tablespoons vegetable oil in 10-inch skillet over medium heat. Cook beef in oil until brown on both sides. Mix remaining ingredients in 3½- to 6-quart slow cooker; add beef. Cover and cook on low heat setting 8 to 10 hours. Continue as directed in step 3.

Chicken and Broth

Prep Time: 25 min

Start to Finish: 1 hr 25 min

About 4 cups broth and 2½ to
3 cups chicken

3- to 3½-lb cut-up broiler-fryer
   chicken*
4½ cups cold water
1 teaspoon salt
½ teaspoon pepper
1 medium stalk celery with leaves,
   cut up
1 medium carrot, cut up
1 small onion, cut up
1 sprig parsley

1. Remove any excess fat from chicken. In 4-quart Dutch oven or stockpot, place chicken, giblets (except liver) and neck. Add remaining ingredients; heat to boiling. Skim foam from broth; reduce heat. Cover and simmer about 45 minutes or until juice of chicken is clear when thickest piece is cut to bone (170°F for breasts; 180°F for thighs and drumsticks).

2. Remove chicken from broth. Cool chicken about 10 minutes or just until cool enough to handle. Strain broth through cheesecloth-lined sieve; discard vegetables.

3. Remove skin and bones from chicken. Cut chicken into ½-inch pieces. Skim fat from broth. Use broth and chicken immediately, or cover and refrigerate broth and chicken in separate containers up to 24 hours or freeze for up to 6 months.

*3 to 3½ pounds chicken necks, backs and giblets (except liver) can be used to make broth.

Slow Cooker Directions: Decrease water to 3 cups. Increase salt to 1¼ teaspoons. Mix all ingredients in 3½- to 6-quart slow cooker. Cover and cook on low heat setting 8 to 10 hours or until juice of chicken is clear when thickest piece is cut to bone. Continue as directed in step 2.

Quick Broth Alternatives

If you don't have time to make your own broth, try one of these quick alternatives:

Ready-to-serve broth: 1 can (14.5 oz) chicken, beef or vegetable broth equals about 1¾ cups broth.

Condensed broth: 1 can (10.5 oz) condensed chicken or beef broth diluted with 1 soup can water equals 2⅔ cups broth.

Bouillon: 1 chicken, beef or vegetable bouillon cube or 1 teaspoon bouillon granules mixed with 1 cup water equals 1 cup broth.

Broth or stock base: Follow directions on container; each brand is different.

Fish Broth

Prep Time: 20 min
Start to Finish: 1 hr
About 6 cups

1 ½ lb fish bones and trimmings
4 cups cold water
2 cups dry white wine or clam juice
1 tablespoon lemon juice
1 teaspoon salt
½ teaspoon dried thyme leaves
1 large celery stalk with leaves, chopped
1 small onion, sliced
3 medium mushrooms, chopped
3 sprigs parsley
1 bay leaf

1. Rinse fish bones and trimmings with cold water; drain. In 4-quart Dutch oven or stockpot, mix bones, trimmings, 4 cups cold water and remaining ingredients; heat to boiling. Skim foam from broth; reduce heat. Cover and simmer 30 minutes.

2. Cool about 10 minutes. Strain broth through cheesecloth-lined sieve; discard skin, bones, vegetables and seasonings. Use broth immediately, or cover and refrigerate up to 24 hours or freeze up to 6 months.

Vegetable Broth

Prep Time: 20 min
Start to Finish: 1 hr 30 min
About 8 cups

6 cups coarsely chopped mild vegetables (bell peppers, carrots, celery, leeks, mushroom stems, potatoes, spinach, zucchini)
1 medium onion, coarsely chopped (½ cup)
½ cup parsley sprigs
8 cups cold water
2 tablespoons chopped fresh or 2 teaspoons dried basil leaves
2 tablespoons chopped fresh or 2 teaspoons dried thyme leaves
1 teaspoon salt
¼ teaspoon cracked black pepper
4 cloves garlic, finely chopped
2 bay leaves

1. In 4-quart Dutch oven or stockpot, heat all ingredients to boiling; reduce heat. Cover and simmer 1 hour, stirring occasionally.

2. Cool about 10 minutes. Strain broth through cheesecloth-lined sieve; discard vegetables and seasonings. Use broth immediately, or cover and refrigerate up to 24 hours or freeze for up to 6 months. Stir before measuring.

Soup for Dessert!

Santa Fe Melon Soup

Prep Time: 15 min
Start to Finish: 15 min
6 Servings (about ⅔ cup each)

1 large cantaloupe, peeled, seeded
    and chopped (4 pounds)
3 tablespoons sugar
2 tablespoons chopped fresh mint
    leaves
½ cup sour cream
¼ cup dry white wine or white grape
    juice
2 teaspoons grated orange peel
Fresh mint leaf

1.   In food processor or blender,
place cantaloupe, sugar and
2 tablespoons mint. Cover and
process until smooth.

2.   Stir together cantaloupe, sour
cream, wine and orange peel.
Garnish with mint leaves.

Serve this refreshingly delicious
    soup in hollowed-out cantaloupe
    halves or even tall margarita
    glasses. Make fun cactus
    garnishes by cutting shapes from
    the cantaloupe rind.

Chilled Berry Soup

Prep Time: 5 min
Start to Finish: 5 min
3 Servings (¾ cup each)

1 cup vanilla-flavored soymilk
2 cups frozen organic unsweetened
    strawberries, partially thawed
⅓ cup orange juice
2 tablespoons sugar
Sliced fresh strawberries, if desired
Fresh mint sprigs, if desired

1.   In blender or food processor,
place soymilk, frozen strawberries,
orange juice and sugar. Cover; blend
on high speed about 30 seconds or
until smooth.

2.   Pour into 3 individual serving
bowls; top with sliced fresh
strawberries and mint.

Just for fun, serve this soup
    with "cake croutons." In 10-inch
    nonstick skillet, melt 1 tablespoon
    butter or trans-fat free margarine
    over medium-high heat; add 1 cup
    ¾-inch cubes angel food cake.
    Cook, stirring constantly, until
    light brown.

1

meaty
soups

Steak and Potato Soup

Prep Time: 45 min ▪ Start to Finish: 45 min ▪ 10 Servings

2-lb boneless beef sirloin steak (1 inch thick)

2 tablespoons vegetable oil

1½ cups coarsely chopped onions

3 cloves garlic, finely chopped

2 lb small red potatoes, cut into ¾-inch pieces

3 cups ready-to-eat baby-cut carrots, cut lengthwise into fourths

1 bag (1 lb) frozen cut green beans

2 tablespoons chopped fresh or 2 teaspoons dried basil leaves

½ teaspoon freshly ground black pepper

6 cans (14 oz each) beef broth

3 tablespoons steak sauce

1 Cut beef into ¼-inch strips; cut strips into 1-inch pieces. In 8-quart stockpot or Dutch oven, heat oil over medium-high heat. Cook and stir beef in oil 4 to 5 minutes or until brown; add onion and garlic. Cook and stir 2 minutes.

2 Stir in remaining ingredients. Heat to boiling; reduce heat to low. Cover and simmer 12 to 15 minutes, stirring occasionally, until vegetables are tender.

1 Serving: Calories 330 (Calories from Fat 90); Total Fat 10g (Saturated Fat 3g); Cholesterol 80mg; Sodium 960mg; Total Carbohydrate 28g (Dietary Fiber 4g); Protein 33g

It's a snap to cut the steak into slices of even thickness if you pop it into the freezer for about 20 minutes first.

Beef 'n Veggie Soup with Mozzarella

Prep Time: 25 min ▮ Start to Finish: 25 min ▮ 8 Servings

1 lb lean (at least 80%) ground beef
1 large onion, chopped (1 cup)
2 cups frozen mixed vegetables (from 1-lb bag)
1 can (14.5 oz) diced tomatoes with green pepper, celery and onions (or other variety), undrained
4 cups water
5 teaspoons beef bouillon granules
1½ teaspoons Italian seasoning
¼ teaspoon pepper
1 cup shredded mozzarella cheese (4 oz)

1 In 4-quart Dutch oven, cook beef and onion over medium-high heat 5 to 7 minutes, stirring occasionally, until beef is brown; drain.

2 Stir in remaining ingredients except cheese. Heat to boiling; reduce heat. Simmer uncovered 6 to 8 minutes, stirring occasionally, until vegetables are tender.

3 In each of 8 soup bowls, sprinkle about 2 tablespoons cheese; fill bowls with soup.

1 Serving: Calories 200 (Calories from Fat 80); Total Fat 9g (Saturated Fat 5g); Cholesterol 45mg; Sodium 790mg; Total Carbohydrate 13g (Dietary Fiber 3g); Protein 16g

For a fabulous and filling supper, add some hearty rustic sourdough or Italian rolls for dipping into the soup and a Caesar salad kit for chilly, crunchy goodness.

Asian Beef and Noodle Soup

Prep Time: 1 hr 10 min ▪ Start to Finish: 1 hr 10 min ▪ 6 Servings

3 oz uncooked cellophane noodles
(bean threads)
1 tablespoon dark sesame oil
1½ lb boneless beef top sirloin steak,
cut into bite-size strips
2 teaspoons finely chopped garlic
2 packages (3.5 oz each) fresh shiitake
or button mushrooms, sliced
6 cups beef broth

2 cups finely sliced bok choy
1 cup julienne strips (matchstick-size)
carrots
½ teaspoon salt
½ teaspoon ground ginger
⅛ teaspoon pepper
2 medium green onions, sliced
(2 tablespoons)

1 In medium bowl, soak bundle of cellophane noodles in warm water 10 to 15 minutes or until softened; drain. Cut noodle bundle into thirds. Cover and set aside.

2 In 5- to 6-quart Dutch oven, heat oil over medium-high heat. Cook beef, garlic and mushrooms in oil 5 to 6 minutes, stirring occasionally, just until beef is no longer pink.

3 Stir in remaining ingredients except noodles and onions. Heat to boiling; reduce heat to medium-low. Cover and cook 14 to 15 minutes, stirring occasionally, until beef is tender.

4 Stir in noodles. Cover and cook 2 to 3 minutes or until noodles are hot. Sprinkle with onions.

1 Serving: Calories 235 (Calories from Fat 65); Total Fat 7g (Saturated Fat 2g); Cholesterol 60mg; Sodium 1300mg; Total Carbohydrate 14g (Dietary Fiber 2g); Protein 28g

A salad of pink grapefruit sections, sliced seeded cucumbers and sliced celery tossed with your favorite Asian dressing goes great with this noodle soup dinner. Try topping the salad with rice crackers for extra crunch.

Burger Beef Soup

Prep Time: 30 min ▪ Start to Finish: 30 min ▪ 4 Servings

1 lb lean (at least 80%) ground beef
1 small onion, chopped (¼ cup)
1 can (10.75 oz) condensed cream of celery soup
½ cup frozen sweet peas (from 1-lb bag)
2 cups tomato juice
1¼ cups water
¾ teaspoon chopped fresh or ¼ teaspoon dried basil leaves
¾ teaspoon chopped fresh or ¼ teaspoon dried marjoram leaves
⅛ teaspoon pepper
1 dried bay leaf
1 cup uncooked egg noodles (2 oz)

1 In 4-quart Dutch oven, cook beef and onion over medium heat 8 to 10 minutes, stirring occasionally, until beef is brown; drain.

2 Stir in remaining ingredients except noodles. Heat to boiling. Stir in noodles; reduce heat. Simmer uncovered about 10 minutes, stirring occasionally, until noodles are tender. Remove bay leaf.

1 Serving: Calories 390 (Calories from Fat 190); Total Fat 21g (Saturated Fat 8g); Cholesterol 80mg; Sodium 1060mg; Total Carbohydrate 24g (Dietary Fiber 3g); Protein 26g

Kids will love this soup when it's served with fruity gelatin salad along with carrot and celery sticks with ranch dressing to dip them in.

Cheesy Lasagna Soup

Prep Time: 40 min ▮ Start to Finish: 40 min ▮ 6 Servings

1 lb lean ground beef
1 medium onion, sliced
2 large green bell peppers, cut into
    1-inch pieces
2 cloves garlic, finely chopped
2 cups water
2 cans (14.5 oz each) diced tomatoes
    in olive oil, garlic and spices,
    undrained
1 can (6 oz) tomato paste

2 cups uncooked mini lasagna
    (mafalda) noodles or wide egg
    noodles (4 oz)
1 tablespoon packed brown sugar
1½ teaspoons Italian seasoning,
    crumbled
¼ teaspoon pepper
1½ cups Italian-style croutons
1½ cups shredded part-skim
    mozzarella cheese (6 oz)

1 In 4-quart Dutch oven, cook beef, onion, bell peppers and garlic over medium heat 8 to 10 minutes, stirring occasionally, until beef is brown and onion is tender; drain. Stir water, diced tomatoes and tomato paste into beef mixture.

2 Stir in remaining ingredients except croutons and cheese. Heat to boiling; reduce heat to low. Cover and simmer about 10 minutes, stirring occasionally, until pasta is tender.

3 Set oven control to broil. Pour hot soup into 6 ovenproof soup bowls or casseroles (do not use glass). Top each with ¼ cup croutons. Sprinkle with cheese. With tops 3 to 4 inches from heat, broil soup 1 to 2 minutes or until cheese is melted.

1 Serving: Calories 450 (Calories from Fat 160); Total Fat 18g (Saturated Fat 8g); Cholesterol 70mg; Sodium 910mg; Total Carbohydrate 40g (Dietary Fiber 5g); Protein 27g

Instead of using your broiler to melt the cheese, why not let the hot soup melt the cheese on its own? It cuts down on prep time, and kids will love the ooey-gooey strings of cheese that form as a result.

Minestrone with Italian Sausage

Prep Time: 45 min ▪ Start to Finish: 45 min ▪ 7 Servings

1 tablespoon olive or vegetable oil

1 lb bulk sweet Italian sausage

1 medium onion, chopped (½ cup)

2 medium carrots, coarsely chopped (1 cup)

2 teaspoons dried basil leaves

2 teaspoons finely chopped garlic

3 cans (14 oz each) beef broth

1 can (14.5 oz) diced tomatoes, undrained

1 can (15.5 oz) great northern beans, rinsed and drained

1 cup uncooked small elbow macaroni (3½ oz)

1 medium zucchini, cut lengthwise in half, then cut into ¼-inch slices (1 cup)

1 cup frozen cut green beans (from 1-lb bag)

1 In 5-quart Dutch oven, heat oil over medium-high heat. Cook sausage, onion, carrots, basil and garlic in oil 5 to 7 minutes, stirring frequently, until sausage is no longer pink; drain.

2 Stir broth, tomatoes and great northern beans into sausage mixture. Heat to boiling; reduce heat to medium-low. Cover and cook 7 to 8 minutes, stirring occasionally.

3 Stir in macaroni, zucchini and frozen green beans; heat to boiling. Cook over medium-high heat 5 to 6 minutes, stirring occasionally, until vegetables are hot and macaroni is tender.

1 Serving: Calories 345 (Calories from Fat 135); Total Fat 15g (Saturated Fat 5g); Cholesterol 35mg; Sodium 1060mg; Total Carbohydrate 37g (Dietary Fiber 6g); Protein 21g

Make it meatless! Simply substitute an additional can of great northern beans or your favorite canned beans for the sausage and use vegetable broth instead of beef broth.

Creamy Beef, Mushroom and Noodle Soup

Prep Time: 1 hr ▪ Start to Finish: 1 hr ▪ 7 Servings

2 tablespoons butter or margarine
1 medium onion, coarsely chopped (½ cup)
2 teaspoons finely chopped garlic
1 package (8 oz) sliced fresh mushrooms
1½ lb boneless beef top sirloin steak, cut into 2×¾×¼-inch pieces
6 cups beef broth
½ cup dry sherry or beef broth
¼ cup ketchup
¾ teaspoon salt
⅛ teaspoon pepper
2 cups uncooked medium egg noodles
1 container (8 oz) sour cream

1 In 5- to 6-quart Dutch oven, melt butter over medium-high heat. Cook onion, garlic and mushrooms in butter 5 to 6 minutes, stirring frequently, until mushrooms are softened.

2 Stir in beef. Cook 5 to 6 minutes, stirring frequently, until beef is no longer pink. Stir in remaining ingredients except noodles and sour cream. Heat to boiling; reduce heat to medium-low. Cover and cook 10 minutes, stirring occasionally. Stir in noodles. Cover and cook 5 to 7 minutes, stirring occasionally, until noodles are tender.

3 Stir in sour cream. Cook 3 to 5 minutes, stirring frequently, until well blended.

1 Serving: Calories 290 (Calories from Fat 125); Total Fat 14g (Saturated Fat 7g); Cholesterol 90mg; Sodium 1100mg; Total Carbohydrate 15g (Dietary Fiber 1g); Protein 26g

More than a soup, this hearty meal-in-a-bowl goes well with breadsticks and a side of steamed broccoli.

Borscht

Prep Time: 1 hr ▪ Start to Finish: 4 hr ▪ 6 Servings

¾ lb boneless beef chuck, tip or round, cut into ½-inch cubes

1 smoked pork hock

4 cups water

1 can (10.5 oz) condensed beef broth

1 teaspoon salt

¼ teaspoon pepper

4 medium beets, cooked, or 1 can (15 oz) sliced beets, drained

1 large onion, sliced

2 cloves garlic, finely chopped

2 medium potatoes, cubed (2 cups)

3 cups shredded cabbage

2 teaspoons dill seed or 1 sprig dill weed

1 tablespoon mixed pickling spice

¼ cup red wine vinegar

¾ cup sour cream

Chopped fresh dill weed, if desired

1 In 4-quart Dutch oven, heat beef, pork hock, water, broth, salt and pepper to boiling; reduce heat. Cover and simmer 1 hour to 1 hour 30 minutes or until beef is tender.

2 Shred beets, or cut into ¼-inch strips. Remove pork from soup; let stand until cool enough to handle. Remove pork from bone; cut pork into bite-size pieces.

3 Stir pork, beets, onion, garlic, potatoes and cabbage into soup. Tie dill seed and pickling spice in cheesecloth bag or place in tea ball; add to soup. Cover and simmer 2 hours.

4 Stir in vinegar. Simmer uncovered 10 minutes. Remove spice bag. Serve sour cream with soup. Sprinkle with chopped dill weed.

1 Serving: Calories 275 (Calories from Fat 115); Total Fat 13g (Saturated Fat 6g); Cholesterol 60mg; Sodium 800mg; Total Carbohydrate 22g (Dietary Fiber 3g); Protein 20g

Asian Pork and Noodle Soup

Prep Time: 30 min ▪ Start to Finish: 30 min ▪ 5 Servings

1 lb boneless pork sirloin or loin, cut into ½-inch pieces
2 cloves garlic, finely chopped
2 teaspoons finely chopped gingerroot
2 cans (14 oz each) chicken broth
2 cups water
2 tablespoons soy sauce
2 cups uncooked fine egg noodles (4 oz)
1 medium carrot, sliced (½ cup)
1 small red bell pepper, chopped (½ cup)
2 cups fresh spinach leaves

1 Spray 3-quart saucepan with cooking spray; heat over medium-high heat. Add pork, garlic and gingerroot; cook 3 to 5 minutes, stirring frequently, or until pork is brown.

2 Stir in broth, water and soy sauce. Heat to boiling; reduce heat. Simmer uncovered 5 minutes. Stir in noodles, carrot and bell pepper. Simmer uncovered about 10 minutes or until noodles are tender.

3 Stir in spinach; cook until thoroughly heated.

1 Serving: Calories 260 (Calories from Fat 80); Total Fat 9g (Saturated Fat 3g); Cholesterol 75mg; Sodium 1100mg; Total Carbohydrate 19g (Dietary Fiber 2g); Protein 26g

Speed it up! For this recipe, instead of cutting the pork yourself, buy pork chow mein meat, which is already cut up and ready to go.

Thai-Style Chicken Curry Soup

Prep Time: 15 min ▪ Start to Finish: 15 min ▪ 4 Servings

1 carton (32 oz) chicken broth
3 tablespoons packed brown sugar
2 tablespoons soy sauce
2 tablespoons rice vinegar
2 teaspoons curry powder
1 small red bell pepper, coarsely chopped (½ cup)
1 small jalapeño chile, seeded, finely chopped (1 tablespoon)
2 cups chopped deli rotisserie chicken (from 2- to 2½-lb chicken)
2 tablespoons chopped fresh cilantro, if desired

1 In 3-quart saucepan, stir all ingredients except chicken and cilantro. Heat to boiling over medium-high heat. Reduce heat to medium. Simmer uncovered 3 to 5 minutes or until bell pepper is crisp-tender.

2 Stir in chicken. Cook 1 to 2 minutes or until chicken is hot. Just before serving, add cilantro.

1 Serving: Calories 210 (Calories from Fat 60); Total Fat 7g (Saturated Fat 2g); Cholesterol 60mg; Sodium 1770mg; Total Carbohydrate 14g (Dietary Fiber 0g); Protein 25g

Like spicy food? Add an additional tablespoon of finely chopped jalapeño chile.

Chicken Tortilla Soup

Prep Time: 35 min ▪ Start to Finish: 35 min ▪ 6 Servings

1 carton (32 oz) chicken broth
1 cup chunky-style salsa (from 16-oz jar)
2 cups shredded deli rotisserie chicken (from 2- to 2½-lb chicken)
¾ cup crushed tortilla chips
1 medium avocado, pitted, peeled and chopped
1½ cups shredded Monterey Jack cheese (6 oz)
2 tablespoons chopped fresh cilantro
Lime wedges, if desired

1 In 3-quart saucepan, heat broth, salsa and chicken to boiling over medium-high heat, stirring occasionally.

2 Meanwhile, divide crushed chips among 6 serving bowls. Spoon hot soup over chips, then top with avocado, cheese and cilantro. Serve with lime wedges.

1 Serving: Calories 330 (Calories from Fat 180); Total Fat 20g (Saturated Fat 8g); Cholesterol 65mg; Sodium 1390mg; Total Carbohydrate 13g (Dietary Fiber 2g); Protein 24g

Adjust the heat level to individual tastes by choosing mild or medium salsa.

Chicken Creole Soup

Prep Time: 1 hr 20 min ▪ Start to Finish: 1 hr 20 min ▪ 8 Servings

2 tablespoons butter or margarine
2 medium onions, coarsely chopped (1 cup)
2 medium stalks celery, coarsely chopped (1 cup)
1 medium green bell pepper, coarsely chopped (1 cup)
2 teaspoons finely chopped garlic
2½ lb boneless skinless chicken breasts or thighs, cut into 1-inch pieces
¼ cup all-purpose flour
4 cups chicken broth
2 cans (14.5 oz each) diced tomatoes, undrained
2 dried bay leaves
1 teaspoon salt
¼ teaspoon ground red pepper (cayenne)
1 cup uncooked regular long-grain rice
2 cups water

1 In 5- to 6-quart Dutch oven, melt butter over medium-high heat. Cook onions, celery, bell pepper, garlic and chicken in butter 7 to 9 minutes, stirring frequently, until onion is softened and chicken is no longer pink in center.

2 Stir in flour. Cook 5 to 6 minutes, stirring constantly, until flour is light brown. Stir in remaining ingredients except rice and water. Heat to boiling; reduce heat to medium-low.

3 Cover and cook 25 to 30 minutes, stirring occasionally, until chicken is tender. Meanwhile, cook rice in water as directed on package; stir cooked rice into soup. Remove bay leaves.

1 Serving: Calories 345 (Calories from Fat 70); Total Fat 8g (Saturated Fat 3g); Cholesterol 95mg; Sodium 810mg; Total Carbohydrate 32g (Dietary Fiber 2g); Protein 36g

Chicken Noodle Soup

Prep Time: 25 min ▪ Start to Finish: 25 min ▪ 4 Servings

1 tablespoon olive or vegetable oil
2 cloves garlic, finely chopped
8 medium green onions, sliced (½ cup)
2 medium carrots, chopped (1 cup)
2 cups cubed deli rotisserie chicken (from 2- to 2½-lb chicken)
2 cups uncooked egg noodles (4 oz)
1 tablespoon chopped fresh parsley or 1 teaspoon parsley flakes
¼ teaspoon pepper
1 dried bay leaf
3 cans (14 oz each) chicken broth

1 In 3-quart saucepan, heat oil over medium heat. Cook garlic, onions and carrots in oil 4 minutes, stirring occasionally.

2 Stir in remaining ingredients. Heat to boiling; reduce heat. Cover; simmer about 10 minutes, stirring occasionally, until carrots and noodles are tender. Remove bay leaf.

1 Serving: Calories 320 (Calories from Fat 100); Total Fat 11g (Saturated Fat 3g); Cholesterol 85mg; Sodium 1630mg; Total Carbohydrate 24g (Dietary Fiber 2g); Protein 30g

Running short of time? Use shredded or julienne-cut carrots from a bag.

Noodle and Chicken Bowls

Prep Time: 15 min ▪ Start to Finish: 15 min ▪ 4 Servings

4 cups water

2 packages (3 oz each) Oriental-flavor ramen noodle soup mix

1 cup fresh spinach leaves, torn into bite-size pieces

2 oz fresh snow pea pods, strings removed, cut in half crosswise (½ cup)

½ cup shredded or julienne-cut carrots

1 can (8 oz) sliced water chestnuts, drained

1 teaspoon sesame oil

1½ cups chopped deli rotisserie chicken (from 2- to 2½-lb chicken)

2 medium green onions, chopped (2 tablespoons)

1 In 3-quart saucepan, heat water to boiling over medium-high heat. Add noodles (breaking apart if desired), spinach, pea pods, carrots and water chestnuts. Cook 3 minutes, stirring occasionally.

2 Stir in seasoning packets from soup mixes, sesame oil, chicken and onions. Cook 1 to 2 minutes or until chicken is hot.

1 Serving: Calories 330 (Calories from Fat 120); Total Fat 13g (Saturated Fat 4g); Cholesterol 45mg; Sodium 940mg; Total Carbohydrate 34g (Dietary Fiber 4g); Protein 20g

Scatter chopped fresh basil, mint and/or cilantro over the soup just before serving for a fresh taste reminiscent of Vietnamese pho noodle bowls.

Chicken-Vegetable Pot Pie Soup

Prep Time: 1 hr ■ Start to Finish: 1 hr ■ 6 Servings

1 sheet frozen puff pastry (from 17.3-oz package), thawed
2 tablespoons butter or margarine
6 small red potatoes, cut into eighths
1 medium stalk celery, coarsely chopped (½ cup)
1 medium carrot, coarsely chopped (½ cup)
1 small onion, coarsely chopped (¼ cup)
5 cups chicken broth

¼ cup quick-mixing flour
1 teaspoon poultry seasoning
¼ teaspoon salt
⅛ teaspoon pepper
2½ cups 1-inch pieces deli rotisserie chicken (from 2- to 2½-lb chicken)
1 cup frozen sweet peas (from 1-lb bag)
¼ cup whipping cream

1 Heat oven to 400°F. Cut 6 rounds from puff pastry with 3-inch round cutter. Place on ungreased cookie sheet. Bake 12 to 15 minutes or until puffed and golden brown. Keep warm.

2 Meanwhile, in 4½- to 5-quart Dutch oven, melt butter over medium-high heat. Cook potatoes, celery, carrot and onion in butter 5 to 6 minutes, stirring frequently, until onion is softened.

3 Beat broth, flour, poultry seasoning, salt and pepper into potato mixture with wire whisk. Heat to boiling; reduce heat to medium-low. Cover; cook 15 to 20 minutes, stirring occasionally, until potatoes are tender and soup is slightly thickened.

4 Stir in remaining ingredients. Cover; cook 5 to 6 minutes, stirring occasionally, until chicken and peas are hot. Ladle soup into bowls; top each serving with pastry.

1 Serving: Calories 340 (Calories from Fat 120); Total Fat 13g (Saturated Fat 6g); Cholesterol 75mg; Sodium 1310mg; Total Carbohydrate 32g (Dietary Fiber 4g); Protein 25g

Save time! Pick up the small amounts of carrot and celery at the salad bar in your grocery store.

Homemade Turkey Soup

Prep Time: 1 hr 25 min ▪ Start to Finish: 2 hr 55 min ▪ 10 Servings

Carcass from cooked 10- to 12-lb
    turkey
3 quarts (12 cups) water
1 teaspoon salt
½ teaspoon pepper
¼ teaspoon poultry seasoning or
    dried sage leaves
1 dried bay leaf

½ cup uncooked pearl barley
3 medium carrots, sliced (1½ cups)
1 large onion, chopped (1 cup)
2 medium stalks celery, sliced (1 cup)
3 cups cut-up cooked turkey
2 tablespoons chopped fresh
    parsley, if desired

1 Break up turkey carcass to fit 6-quart Dutch oven. Add water, salt, pepper, poultry seasoning and bay leaf. Heat to boiling over high heat; reduce heat to low. Cover; simmer 1 hour 30 minutes.

2 Skim off any residue that rises to the surface. Remove bones, meat and bay leaf from broth; cool. When cool enough to handle, remove meat from bones and cut into bite-size pieces; set aside. Discard bones and bay leaf.

3 Skim fat from broth; discard. Add turkey meat cut from bones to broth; stir in barley. Heat to boiling; reduce heat to low. Cover; simmer 30 minutes, stirring occasionally.

4 Stir in carrots, onion, celery and 3 cups cooked turkey. Simmer uncovered 20 to 25 minutes longer, stirring occasionally, until vegetables and barley are tender. Stir in parsley.

1 Serving: Calories 140 (Calories from Fat 30); Total Fat 4g (Saturated Fat 1g); Cholesterol 40mg; Sodium 330mg; Total Carbohydrate 13g (Dietary Fiber 3g); Protein 15g

Stir in the veggies! Add up to 3 cups raw or cooked vegetables, such as whole kernel corn, green peas, diced potatoes, sliced zucchini, sliced mushrooms or any combination, along with the carrots, onion and celery.

Turkey-Ginger Tortellini Soup

Prep Time: 35 min ▪ Start to Finish: 35 min ▪ 4 Servings

1 package (7 oz) dried cheese-filled tortellini
2¼ cups water
2 tablespoons rice wine or white wine vinegar
2 tablespoons soy sauce
1 can (10.5 oz) condensed chicken broth
1 to 2 tablespoons finely chopped fresh gingerroot or
    1 to 2 teaspoons ground ginger
2 cups sliced bok choy (stems and leaves)
2 cups cut-up cooked turkey
2 green onions, sliced
1 cup enoki mushrooms (3½ oz)

1 In 3-quart saucepan, cook and drain tortellini as directed on package; set aside. In the same saucepan, heat water, vinegar, soy sauce, broth and gingerroot to boiling; reduce heat to low.

2 Stir bok choy stems (reserve leaves), turkey and onions into saucepan. Simmer uncovered 15 minutes. Stir in bok choy leaves, mushrooms and tortellini. Simmer just until leaves are wilted.

1 Serving: Calories 235 (Calories from Fat 80); Total Fat 9g (Saturated Fat 3g); Cholesterol 100mg; Sodium 830mg; Total Carbohydrate 12g (Dietary Fiber 1g); Protein 26g

Finely chopping the fresh ginger takes a bit more time than using ginger from a can, but the extra flavor is worth it. It's hard to believe those gnarled-looking roots you see at the grocery store taste so sweet and delicious.

Turkey-Spaetzle Soup

Prep Time: 35 min ▪ Start to Finish: 35 min ▪ 6 Servings

2 tablespoons vegetable oil
1 large onion, finely chopped (1 cup)
1 medium carrot, finely chopped (½ cup)
1 medium stalk celery, finely chopped (½ cup)
1 clove garlic, finely chopped
¼ cup all-purpose flour
2 teaspoons dried thyme leaves
¼ teaspoon pepper
2 cups diced cooked turkey
1 can (49.5 oz) chicken broth (6 cups)
1 bag (12 oz) frozen spaetzle
Chopped fresh parsley, if desired

1 In 4-quart saucepan, heat oil over medium-high heat. Add onion, carrot, celery and garlic; cook about 2 minutes, stirring frequently, until crisp-tender.

2 Gradually stir in flour, thyme and pepper; cook about 1 minute, stirring constantly. Stir in turkey and broth; heat to boiling.

3 Stir in frozen spaetzle. Cook 2 to 3 minutes, stirring occasionally, until spaetzle are tender. Sprinkle with parsley.

1 Serving: Calories 240 (Calories from Fat 90); Total Fat 10g (Saturated Fat 3g); Cholesterol 70mg; Sodium 1180mg; Total Carbohydrate 17g (Dietary Fiber 2g); Protein 21g

Spaetzle are tiny egg noodles that are firm enough to use in soup. They have a rich eggy flavor. If you prefer, substitute 3 cups frozen egg noodles (from a 16-ounce bag) for the spaetzle.

2

vegetable, bean & grain soups

Italian Tomato Soup with Pesto-Cheese Toasts

Prep Time: 15 min ■ Start to Finish: 15 min ■ 4 Servings

1 cup water
2 cans (14 oz each) diced tomatoes with Italian herbs, undrained
1 can (11.5 oz) tomato juice
4 slices rosemary, Italian or French bread, ½ inch thick
2 tablespoons basil pesto
2 tablespoons shredded Parmesan cheese

1 In 3-quart saucepan, heat water, tomatoes and tomato juice to boiling.

2 Set oven control to broil. Place bread on ungreased cookie sheet. Spread with pesto; sprinkle with cheese. With tops 4 to 6 inches from heat, broil 1 to 2 minutes or until edges of bread are golden brown.

3 Into 4 soup bowls, ladle soup. Top each serving with bread slice.

1 Serving: Calories 260 (Calories from Fat 60); Total Fat 7g (Saturated Fat 2g); Cholesterol 0mg; Sodium 910mg; Total Carbohydrate 39g (Dietary Fiber 4g); Protein 9g

Take creative license! Turn this into a pizza soup by stirring in 1 pound of browned (drained) Italian sausage and a 2½-ounce can of sliced mushrooms (drained) in step one. Add a simple tossed salad with dressing, and you're good to go.

Chunky Tomato Soup

Prep Time: 1 hr 35 min ▪ Start to Finish: 1 hr 35 min ▪ 8 Servings

2 tablespoons olive or vegetable oil
2 cloves garlic, finely chopped
2 medium stalks celery, coarsely chopped (1 cup)
2 medium carrots, coarsely chopped (1 cup)
2 cans (28 oz each) Italian-style (plum) tomatoes, undrained
2 cups water
1 teaspoon dried basil leaves
½ teaspoon pepper
2 cans (14 oz each) chicken broth

1 In 5- to 6-quart Dutch oven, heat oil over medium-high heat. Cook garlic, celery and carrots in oil 5 to 7 minutes, stirring frequently, until carrots are crisp-tender.

2 Stir in tomatoes, breaking up tomatoes coarsely. Stir in water, basil, pepper and broth. Heat to boiling; reduce heat to low.

3 Cover and simmer 1 hour, stirring occasionally.

1 Serving: Calories 95 (Calories from Fat 35); Total Fat 4g (Saturated Fat 1g); Cholesterol 0mg; Sodium 760mg; Total Carbohydrate 11g (Dietary Fiber 3g); Protein 4g

Hot grilled Cheddar cheese sandwiches make a great partner for this veggie soup. Tall glasses of ice-cold milk and a couple of chocolate chip cookies are all you need to serve up lunch!

Spring Onion Soup
with Garlic Croutons

Prep Time: 45 min ▪ Start to Finish: 45 min ▪ 4 Servings

Croutons
3 tablespoons butter or margarine
1 cup ¾-inch cubes day-old French
    bread (crusts removed)
1 teaspoon garlic powder

Soup
3 tablespoons butter or margarine
1 medium white onion, finely
    chopped (½ cup)

4 cups water
2 tablespoons chicken soup base
    (from 8-oz jar)
16 medium green onions, sliced
    (1 cup)
½ teaspoon pepper
4 tablespoons shredded Parmesan
    cheese

1 Heat oven to 375°F. In 15×10-inch pan or cookie sheet with sides, melt 3 tablespoons butter in oven. Add bread cubes and garlic powder to butter; toss well to combine. Bake about 10 minutes, stirring occasionally, until bread cubes are crisp and brown.

2 Meanwhile, in 2-quart saucepan, melt 3 tablespoons butter over medium heat. Add white onion; cook over medium heat 5 to 7 minutes, stirring occasionally, until onion is translucent. Stir in water, soup base, green onions and pepper. Heat to boiling; reduce heat. Simmer uncovered 10 minutes. Stir before serving.

3 Top each serving with ¼ cup croutons and 1 tablespoon cheese.

1 Serving: Calories 240 (Calories from Fat 180); Total Fat 20g (Saturated Fat 12g); Cholesterol 50mg; Sodium 1560mg; Total Carbohydrate 10g (Dietary Fiber 1g); Protein 5g

Prepare early! Make this soup through step two and refrigerate. Then reheat and garnish just in time for the party.

Beer and Cheese Soup

Prep Time: 25 min ▪ Start to Finish: 25 min ▪ 5 Servings

2 tablespoons butter or margarine
2 medium carrots, finely chopped (1 cup)
1 large onion, chopped (1 cup)
1 medium stalk celery, finely chopped (½ cup)
¼ cup all-purpose flour
1 can or bottle (12 oz) beer*
2 cups vegetable broth
½ teaspoon salt
1 cup sour cream
2 cups shredded sharp Cheddar cheese (8 oz)

1 In 3-quart saucepan, melt butter over medium heat. Add carrots, onion and celery; cook, stirring occasionally, until tender.

2 Stir in flour. Gradually stir in beer, broth and salt. Heat to boiling. Reduce heat to low; cover and simmer about 10 minutes or until vegetables are tender.

3 Remove saucepan from heat. Add sour cream and cheese; stir until cheese is melted.

*To substitute for beer, use an additional 1½ cups vegetable broth.

1 Serving: Calories 380 (Calories from Fat 260); Total Fat 29g (Saturated Fat 17g); Cholesterol 90mg; Sodium 990mg; Total Carbohydrate 17g (Dietary Fiber 2g); Protein 14g

Lighten up this favorite chill-chasing soup by using low-fat sour cream and reduced-fat Cheddar cheese instead of the regular versions.

Gazpacho

Prep Time: 20 min ▪ Start to Finish: 1 hr 20 min ▪ 8 Servings

1 can (28 oz) whole tomatoes, undrained
1 medium green bell pepper, finely chopped (1 cup)
1 cup finely chopped cucumber
1 cup croutons
1 medium onion, chopped (½ cup)
2 tablespoons dry white wine or chicken broth
2 tablespoons olive or vegetable oil
1 tablespoon ground cumin
1 tablespoon white vinegar
½ teaspoon salt
¼ teaspoon pepper

1 In blender or food processor, place tomatoes, ½ cup of the bell pepper, ½ cup of the cucumbers, ½ cup of the croutons, ¼ cup of the onion and the remaining ingredients. Cover and blend on medium speed until smooth. Pour into large bowl.

2 Cover and refrigerate at least 1 hour. Serve remaining vegetables and croutons as accompaniments.

1 Serving: Calories 75 (Calories from Fat 35); Total Fat 4g (Saturated Fat 1g); Cholesterol 0mg; Sodium 320mg; Total Carbohydrate 10g (Dietary Fiber 2g); Protein 2g

Ratatouille Soup

Prep Time: 25 min ■ Start to Finish: 25 min ■ 6 Servings

1 tablespoon olive or vegetable oil
1 small onion, chopped (¼ cup)
1 clove garlic, finely chopped
1 small eggplant (1 lb), cut into ½-inch cubes
3 medium tomatoes, coarsely chopped (2¼ cups)
1 medium zucchini, cut into ½-inch slices (2 cups)
1 small green bell pepper, chopped (½ cup)
1 can (10.5 oz) condensed chicken broth
1 broth can water
¼ teaspoon salt
¼ teaspoon pepper

1 In 4-quart Dutch oven, heat oil over medium-high heat. Cook onion and garlic in oil about 3 minutes, stirring occasionally, until onion is tender.

2 Stir in remaining ingredients. Heat to boiling; reduce heat to low. Cover and simmer about 10 minutes or until vegetables are crisp-tender.

1 Serving: Calories 85 (Calories from Fat 25); Total Fat 3g (Saturated Fat 1g); Cholesterol 0mg; Sodium 420mg; Total Carbohydrate 11g (Dietary Fiber 3); Protein 4g

You can throw this hearty dish together in no time when you cut up the veggies the night before.

Minestrone with Garlic Croutons

Prep Time: 45 min ▪ Start to Finish: 45 min ▪ 6 Servings

Croutons

2 cups cubed (½ to ¾ inch) French
  bread

¼ cup butter or margarine, melted

½ teaspoon garlic powder

¼ teaspoon seasoned salt

Soup

1 tablespoon olive or vegetable oil

1½ cups frozen bell pepper and
  onion stir-fry (from 1-lb bag)

2 cups frozen mixed vegetables
  (from 1-lb bag)

2 cans (14.5 oz each) Italian-style
  stewed tomatoes, undrained

2 cans (14 oz each) beef broth

½ cup uncooked small pasta
  shells (2 oz)

1 can (15 oz) dark red kidney beans,
  drained, rinsed

1 Heat oven to 350°F. In medium bowl, mix all crouton ingredients until bread is well coated. In ungreased 15×10-inch pan, spread croutons. Bake 15 to 20 minutes, stirring and turning occasionally, until golden brown and crispy.

2 Meanwhile, in 4-quart saucepan, heat oil over medium-high heat. Add stir-fry vegetables. Cook 3 to 4 minutes, stirring frequently, until tender. Stir in mixed vegetables, tomatoes and broth. Heat to boiling, breaking up tomatoes with spoon as mixture cooks. Stir in pasta. Cook uncovered over medium heat 10 to 12 minutes, stirring occasionally, until vegetables and pasta are tender.

3 Stir in beans. Cook 4 to 5 minutes, stirring occasionally, until thoroughly heated. Top each serving with warm croutons.

1 Serving: Calories 350 (Calories from Fat 100); Total Fat 11g (Saturated Fat 5g); Cholesterol 20mg; Sodium 1330mg; Total Carbohydrate 50g (Dietary Fiber 8g); Protein 13g

Fresh croutons are wonderful, but if you don't feel like making them, use purchased garlic or Parmesan croutons instead. For a heartier soup, you can add cooked Italian sausage or diced cooked beef with the beans.

Acorn Squash and Apple Soup

Prep Time: 1 hr ■ Start to Finish: 2 hr 10 min ■ 6 Servings

1 medium acorn or butternut squash (1½ to 2 lb)
2 tablespoons butter or margarine
1 medium yellow onion, sliced (½ cup)
2 medium tart cooking apples (Granny Smith, Greening or Haralson),
    peeled and sliced
1 teaspoon dried thyme leaves
¼ teaspoon dried basil leaves
2 cans (14.5 oz each) chicken broth (4 cups)
½ cup half-and-half
1 teaspoon ground nutmeg
½ teaspoon salt
¼ teaspoon white or black pepper

1 Heat oven to 350°F. Cut squash in half; remove seeds and fibers. In 13×9-inch pan, place squash cut sides up. Pour ¼ inch water into pan. Bake uncovered about 40 minutes or until tender. Cool; remove pulp from rind and set aside.

2 In heavy 3-quart saucepan, melt butter over medium heat. Cook onion in butter 2 to 3 minutes, stirring occasionally, until crisp-tender. Stir in apples, thyme and basil. Cook 2 minutes, stirring constantly. Stir in broth. Heat to boiling; reduce heat. Simmer uncovered 30 minutes.

3 Remove 1 cup apples with slotted spoon; set aside. Place ⅓ of the remaining apple mixture and squash in blender or food processor. Cover and blend on medium speed about 1 minute or until smooth; pour into bowl. Continue to blend in small batches until all soup is pureed.

4 Return blended mixture and 1 cup reserved apples to saucepan. Stir in half-and-half, nutmeg, salt and pepper; heat through.

1 Serving: Calories 155 (Calories from Fat 65); Total Fat 7g (Saturated Fat 4g); Cholesterol 15mg; Sodium 910mg; Total Carbohydrate 20g (Dietary Fiber 2g); Protein 5g

Sweet Potato–Pear Soup

Prep Time: 25 min ▪ Start to Finish: 45 min ▪ 5 Servings

2 teaspoons canola oil
1 small onion, chopped (¼ cup)
1 medium stalk celery, chopped (½ cup)
½ cup apple juice
½ teaspoon dried thyme leaves
½ teaspoon paprika
3 medium dark-orange sweet potatoes (about 1½ lb), peeled, diced (4½ cups)
1 medium pear, peeled, diced (1 cup)
2 cans (14 oz each) reduced-sodium chicken broth
Chopped fresh thyme, if desired

1 In 3-quart saucepan, heat oil over medium heat. Cook onion and celery in oil 4 to 5 minutes, stirring occasionally, until tender.

2 Stir in remaining ingredients except fresh thyme. Heat to boiling; reduce heat. Cover; simmer 15 to 20 minutes or until sweet potato is tender.

3 Into blender or food processor, add half of the soup. Cover; blend on medium speed 1 to 2 minutes or until smooth; return to saucepan. Blend remaining soup. Heat blended soup 1 to 2 minutes or until hot. Garnish with fresh thyme.

1 Serving: Calories 180 (Calories from Fat 20); Total Fat 2g (Saturated Fat 0g); Cholesterol 0mg; Sodium 420mg; Total Carbohydrate 35g (Dietary Fiber 6g); Protein 5g

For a crunchy texture with this smooth soup, add bagel chips, pita chips or oyster crackers. Adding a green salad that includes beans, tomatoes and a sprinkling of cheese, along with a whole-grain breadstick or roll, makes a satisfying meal.

Tortellini Soup

Prep Time: 40 min ▮ Start to Finish: 40 min ▮ 5 Servings

2 tablespoons butter or margarine
1 medium stalk celery, chopped (½ cup)
1 medium carrot, chopped (½ cup)
1 small onion, chopped (¼ cup)
1 clove garlic, finely chopped
6 cups water
2 extra-large vegetarian vegetable bouillon cubes
2½ cups dried cheese-filled tortellini (10 oz)
1 tablespoon chopped fresh parsley
½ teaspoon ground nutmeg
¼ teaspoon pepper
Freshly grated Parmesan cheese, if desired

1 In 4-quart Dutch oven, melt butter over medium heat. Add celery, carrot, onion and garlic; cook, stirring frequently, until crisp-tender.

2 Stir in water and bouillon cubes. Heat to boiling. Reduce heat to low; stir in tortellini. Cover; simmer about 20 minutes, stirring occasionally, until tortellini are tender.

3 Stir in parsley, nutmeg and pepper. Sprinkle individual servings with cheese.

1 Serving: Calories 280 (Calories from Fat 90); Total Fat 10g (Saturated Fat 5g); Cholesterol 55mg; Sodium 1420mg; Total Carbohydrate 38g (Dietary Fiber 2g); Protein 11g

Tortilla Soup

Prep Time: 15 min ▪ Start to Finish: 35 min ▪ 4 Servings

3 teaspoons vegetable oil
4 corn tortillas (5 or 6 inch), cut into 2×½-inch strips
1 medium onion, chopped (½ cup)
2 cans (14 oz each) vegetable broth
1 can (10 oz) diced tomatoes and green chiles, undrained
1 tablespoon lime juice
1 tablespoon chopped fresh cilantro or parsley

1 In 2-quart nonstick saucepan, heat 2 teaspoons of the oil over medium-high heat. Add tortilla strips; cook 30 to 60 seconds, stirring occasionally, until crisp and light golden brown. Remove from saucepan; drain on paper towels.

2 In same saucepan, cook remaining 1 teaspoon oil and the onion over medium-high heat, stirring occasionally, until onion is tender.

3 Stir in broth and tomatoes. Heat to boiling. Reduce heat to low; simmer uncovered 20 minutes.

4 Stir in lime juice. Serve soup over tortilla strips; garnish with cilantro.

1 Serving: Calories 110 (Calories from Fat 35); Total Fat 4g (Saturated Fat 1g); Cholesterol 0mg; Sodium 1100mg; Total Carbohydrate 17g (Dietary Fiber 2g); Protein 2g

Hungry for chicken? Cut 2 boneless skinless chicken breasts (about ½ pound) into ¾-inch pieces, then cook it with the onion in step two for about 5 minutes or until chicken is no longer pink in center.

Navy Bean Soup

Prep Time: 1 hr 15 min ▪ Start to Finish: 2 hr 15 min ▪ 6 Servings

1 bag (16 oz) dried navy beans, sorted, rinsed
8 cups water
½ cup chili sauce
½ teaspoon dried marjoram leaves
2 medium carrots, chopped (1 cup)
1 large onion, chopped (1 cup)
1 medium stalk celery, chopped (½ cup)
1 can (14 oz) vegetable broth
2 tablespoons chopped fresh parsley

1 In 8-quart Dutch oven, heat beans and water to boiling. Boil uncovered 2 minutes. Remove from heat; cover and let stand 1 hour.

2 Stir in remaining ingredients except parsley. Heat to boiling. Reduce heat to low; cover and simmer about 1 hour, stirring occasionally, until beans are tender.

3 Stir in parsley. Cook 2 to 3 minutes.

1 Serving: Calories 300 (Calories from Fat 10); Total Fat 1g (Saturated Fat 0g); Cholesterol 0mg; Sodium 610mg; Total Carbohydrate 56g (Dietary Fiber 14g); Protein 16g

No navy beans? Although they're larger, cannellini or great northern beans can be used instead.

Southwest Black Bean Soup

Prep Time: 15 min ■ Start to Finish: 30 min ■ 6 Servings

1 tablespoon olive or canola oil

1 medium onion, chopped

2 cloves garlic, finely chopped

1 to 2 jalapeño chiles, seeded, finely chopped

2 cans (15 oz each) black beans, rinsed, drained

1 can (14.5 oz) organic diced or fire-roasted diced tomatoes, undrained

1 can (14 oz) reduced-sodium chicken or vegetable broth

2 teaspoons ground cumin

2 tablespoons chopped fresh cilantro

Plain yogurt or reduced-fat sour cream, if desired

Lime wedges, if desired

1 In 4-quart saucepan, heat oil over medium heat. Add onion, garlic and chiles; cook 3 to 4 minutes, stirring occasionally, until tender.

2 Stir in beans, tomatoes, broth and cumin. Heat to boiling over high heat. Reduce heat to medium-low; cover and simmer 15 minutes. Remove from heat. Using a potato masher, mash beans until soup reaches desired consistency. Stir in cilantro. Top individual servings with yogurt; serve with lime wedges.

1 Serving: Calories 240 (Calories from Fat 30); Total Fat 3g (Saturated Fat 0g); Cholesterol 0mg; Sodium 470mg; Total Carbohydrate 41g (Dietary Fiber 14g); Protein 12g

Black beans are loaded with fiber—the soluble kind that helps to lower blood cholesterol.

Squash and Lentil Bisque

Prep Time: 20 min ■ Start to Finish: 1 hr 15 min ■ 6 Servings

2 medium butternut or acorn squash, cooked and chopped
2 medium green apples, chopped (2 cups)
1 medium red onion, chopped
½ cup unsweetened applesauce
1 cup apple juice
¼ teaspoon ground nutmeg
⅛ teaspoon ground red pepper (cayenne)
1 can (14 oz) vegetable broth
½ cup dried lentils (4 oz), sorted and rinsed
¾ cup shredded reduced-fat mozzarella cheese (3 oz)
6 slices French bread, ¼-inch thick
Additional chopped red onion, if desired

1 In 3-quart saucepan, heat squash, apples, onion, applesauce, apple juice, nutmeg, red pepper and 1 cup of the broth to boiling, stirring occasionally; reduce heat. Cover and simmer 20 minutes.

2 Place squash mixture in blender or food processor. Cover and blend on medium speed until smooth; return mixture to saucepan. Stir in lentils and remaining broth. Heat to boiling; reduce heat. Cover and simmer 25 to 30 minutes, stirring occasionally, until lentils are tender.

3 Set oven control to broil. Sprinkle cheese on bread slices. Place on rack in broiler pan. With tops 3 inches from heat, broil bread about 2 minutes or until cheese is bubbly. Top each serving of soup with slice of cheese bread and chopped onion.

1 Serving: Calories 215 (Calories from Fat 25); Total Fat 3g (Saturated Fat 2g); Cholesterol 10mg; Sodium 420mg; Total Carbohydrate 47g (Dietary Fiber 11g); Protein 11g

Create a sensation by serving this soup in edible squash bowls. Cut butternut or acorn squash in half, and remove seeds and fibers. Cook the squash halves before filling with soup.

Tomato-Lentil Soup

Prep Time: 15 min ▪ Start to Finish: 50 min ▪ 6 Servings

1 tablespoon olive or vegetable oil
1 large onion, finely chopped (1 cup)
1 medium stalk celery, cut into ½-inch pieces
2 cloves garlic, finely chopped
2 medium carrots, cut into ½-inch pieces (1 cup)
1 cup dried lentils (8 oz), sorted, rinsed
4 cups water
2 extra-large vegetarian vegetable bouillon cubes
1 teaspoon dried thyme leaves
¼ teaspoon pepper
1 dried bay leaf
1 can (28 oz) diced tomatoes, undrained

1 In 3-quart saucepan, heat oil over medium-high heat. Add onion, celery and garlic; cook about 5 minutes, stirring occasionally, until softened.

2 Stir in remaining ingredients except tomatoes. Heat to boiling. Reduce heat; cover and simmer 15 to 20 minutes or until lentils and vegetables are tender.

3 Stir in tomatoes. Simmer uncovered about 15 minutes or until heated through. Remove bay leaf before serving.

1 Serving: Calories 200 (Calories from Fat 30); Total Fat 3g (Saturated Fat 0g); Cholesterol 0mg; Sodium 930mg; Total Carbohydrate 33g (Dietary Fiber 9g); Protein 12g

Lots of lentils! Worldwide, hundreds of types of lentils are available in a variety of colors. The most common colors we see are grayish brown, yellow and red. You can use whatever color you like.

Rye Berry Borscht

Prep Time: 30 min ▪ Start to Finish: 10 hr 45 min ▪ 8 servings

1 cup uncooked rye berries
4 cups water
3 cups chopped green cabbage
6 medium beets (about 1¼ lb),
    peeled, chopped (3 cups)
2 medium stalks celery, chopped
    (1 cup)
1 medium potato, peeled, cubed
    (1 cup)
1 medium carrot, chopped (½ cup)
1 medium onion, chopped (½ cup)

2 cloves garlic, finely chopped
1 can (28 oz) diced tomatoes,
    undrained
4 cups water
1 can (19 oz) cannellini beans,
    drained, rinsed
3 tablespoons honey
1½ teaspoons salt
½ teaspoon caraway seed
¼ teaspoon pepper

1 In 5-quart nonstick Dutch oven, soak rye berries in 4 cups water in refrigerator at least 8 hours but no longer than 24 hours.

2 Heat rye berries in water to boiling over high heat. Reduce heat to low. Cover; simmer about 45 minutes or until chewy but tender. Drain.

3 In same Dutch oven, heat cooked rye berries, cabbage, beets, celery, potato, carrot, onion, garlic, tomatoes and 4 cups water to boiling over high heat. Reduce heat to low. Cover; cook 45 minutes.

4 Stir in beans, honey, salt, caraway seed and pepper. Cover; cook 30 to 45 minutes until vegetables are tender.

1 Serving: Calories 350 (Calories from Fat 15); Total Fat 2g (Saturated Fat 0g); Cholesterol 0mg; Sodium 640mg; Total Carbohydrate 69g (Dietary Fiber 7g); Protein 15g

The rye berries are a nice complement to the hardy flavors of the cabbage and beets. Make it easy on yourself by using 3½ cups purchased coleslaw mix in place of the chopped cabbage and carrot.

Creamy Wild Rice Soup

Prep Time: 40 min ▪ Start to Finish: 40 min ▪ 5 Servings

½ cup uncooked wild rice
1¾ cups water
2 tablespoons butter or margarine
2 medium stalks celery, sliced (1 cup)
1 medium carrot, coarsely shredded
    (½ cup)
1 medium onion, chopped (½ cup)
1 small green bell pepper, chopped
    (½ cup)

3 tablespoons all-purpose flour
½ teaspoon salt
¼ teaspoon pepper
1 can (14 oz) vegetable broth
1 cup half-and-half
⅓ cup slivered almonds, toasted*
¼ cup chopped fresh parsley

1 Cook wild rice in 1¼ cups of the water as directed on package.

2 In 3-quart saucepan, melt butter over medium heat. Add celery, carrot, onion and bell pepper; cook, stirring occasionally, until celery is tender.

3 Stir in flour, salt and pepper. Stir in wild rice, remaining ½ cup water and the broth. Heat to boiling. Reduce heat to low; cover and simmer 15 minutes, stirring occasionally.

4 Stir in remaining ingredients. Heat just until hot (do not boil).

*To toast the almonds in the microwave, place ½ teaspoon vegetable oil and the almonds in a 1- or 2-cup glass measuring cup. Microwave uncovered on High 2 minutes 30 seconds to 3 minutes 30 seconds, stirring every 30 seconds, until light brown.

1 Serving: Calories 250 (Calories from Fat 130); Total Fat 15g (Saturated Fat 6g); Cholesterol 30mg; Sodium 660mg; Total Carbohydrate 23g (Dietary Fiber 3g); Protein 6g

Wild rice isn't rice? No, it's an aquatic grass native to North America. The chewy texture of wild rice makes it a perfect meat substitute, but cooked white or brown rice can be used instead.

Oriental Wild Rice Soup

Prep Time: 1 hr 5 min ■ Start to Finish: 1 hr 5 min ■ 4 Servings

½ cup uncooked wild rice
3 cups water
1 small red bell pepper, chopped (½ cup)
1 can (14 oz) vegetable broth
1½ cups sliced fresh mushrooms (4 oz)
1½ cups pieces (½ inch) fresh snow pea pods
3 tablespoons soy sauce
¼ teaspoon garlic powder
¼ teaspoon ground ginger
Chopped fresh cilantro, if desired

1 In 3-quart saucepan, heat wild rice and water to boiling over high heat. Reduce heat to low; cover and simmer 45 minutes, stirring occasionally.

2 Stir in bell pepper and broth. Cook uncovered over medium heat 5 minutes, stirring occasionally.

3 Stir in remaining ingredients except cilantro. Cook uncovered over medium heat 5 to 8 minutes, stirring occasionally, until vegetables are crisp-tender. Sprinkle each serving with cilantro.

1 Serving: Calories 130 (Calories from Fat 0); Total Fat 1g (Saturated Fat 0g); Cholesterol 0mg; Sodium 1130mg; Total Carbohydrate 24g (Dietary Fiber 3g); Protein 6g

For extra flavor, add 1 cup diced cooked chicken or turkey with the remaining ingredients in step three. Complete the meal by serving it with a variety of rice crackers.

satisfying stews

Burgundy Beef Stew

Prep Time: 15 min ▪ Start to Finish: 2 hr 5 min ▪ 8 Servings

6 slices bacon, cut into 1-inch pieces	¼ teaspoon pepper
2 lb beef stew meat, cut into 1-inch pieces	1 clove garlic, finely chopped
½ cup all-purpose flour	1 dried bay leaf
1½ cups dry red wine or beef broth	2 tablespoons butter or margarine
1½ teaspoons chopped fresh or ½ teaspoon dried thyme leaves	1 package (8 oz) sliced fresh mushrooms (3 cups)
1¼ teaspoons salt	4 medium onions, sliced
1 teaspoon beef bouillon granules	Chopped fresh parsley, if desired

1 In 4-quart Dutch oven, cook bacon over low heat, stirring occasionally, until crisp; remove bacon with slotted spoon. Refrigerate bacon.

2 Coat beef with flour. Cook beef in bacon drippings over medium-high heat, stirring frequently, until brown. Drain excess fat from Dutch oven.

3 Add wine and just enough water to cover beef in Dutch oven. Stir in thyme, salt, bouillon granules, pepper, garlic and bay leaf. Heat to boiling; reduce heat. Cover; simmer about 1 hour 30 minutes or until beef is tender.

4 In 12-inch skillet, melt butter over medium heat. Cook mushrooms and onions in butter, stirring frequently, until onions are tender. Stir mushroom mixture and bacon into stew. Cover; simmer 10 minutes. Remove bay leaf. Garnish stew with parsley.

1 Serving: Calories 340 (Calories from Fat 190); Total Fat 21g (Saturated Fat 8g); Cholesterol 85mg; Sodium 650mg; Total Carbohydrate 10g (Dietary Fiber 2g); Protein 27g

Serve the stew over hot cooked egg noodles for a complete meal in a bowl.

Greek Beef and Onion Stew

Prep Time: 40 min ■ Start to Finish: 2 hr 30 min ■ 6 Servings

3 tablespoons olive or vegetable oil
1 medium onion, chopped (½ cup)
2 cloves garlic, finely chopped
2 lb boneless beef chuck, tip or round,
    cut into 1-inch cubes
½ cup dry red wine or water
2 tablespoons red wine vinegar
½ teaspoon salt

¼ teaspoon coarsely ground pepper
1 dried bay leaf
1 stick cinnamon
1 can (8 oz) tomato sauce
1½ lb small white onions, peeled
    (about 12)
Crumbled feta cheese

1 In 4-quart Dutch oven, heat oil over medium heat. Cook chopped onion and garlic in oil, stirring occasionally, until onion is tender. Remove onion and garlic; set aside. Cook beef in remaining oil in Dutch oven about 25 minutes, stirring occasionally, until all liquid has evaporated and beef is brown; drain.

2 Return onion and garlic to Dutch oven. Stir in remaining ingredients except white onions and cheese. Heat to boiling; reduce heat to low. Cover and simmer 1 hour.

3 Stir in white onions. Cover and simmer about 45 minutes or until beef and white onions are tender. Remove bay leaf and cinnamon. Sprinkle with cheese.

1 Serving: Calories 435 (Calories from Fat 215); Total Fat 24g (Saturated Fat 8g); Cholesterol 95mg; Sodium 520mg; Total Carbohydrate 15g (Dietary Fiber 3g); Protein 33g

Pita bread triangles are great for dunking into this flavorful stew, and a bowl of kalamata olives served on the side keeps the Greek theme going.

Italian Beef and Ravioli Stew

Prep Time: 1 hr 40 min ▪ Start to Finish: 1 hr 40 min ▪ 6 Servings

1 tablespoon olive or vegetable oil
1 medium onion, coarsely chopped (½ cup)
2 teaspoons finely chopped garlic
2 teaspoons chopped fresh rosemary leaves
1 medium yellow or green bell pepper, cut into 2-inch strips
2 lb boneless beef chuck, cut into 1-inch pieces
2 cans (14.5 oz each) diced tomatoes with balsamic vinegar, basil and olive oil, undrained
½ cup red wine or beef broth
1½ cups frozen cut green beans (from 1-lb bag)
1 package (9 oz) refrigerated cheese-filled ravioli

1 In 4½- to 5-quart Dutch oven, heat oil over medium-high heat. Cook onion, garlic, rosemary and bell pepper in oil 4 to 5 minutes, stirring frequently, until onions are softened. Stir in beef. Cook 6 to 8 minutes, stirring occasionally, until beef is lightly browned.

2 Stir in tomatoes and wine. Heat to boiling; reduce heat to medium-low. Cover and cook 45 to 50 minutes, stirring occasionally, until beef is tender.

3 Stir in frozen green beans and ravioli. Increase heat to medium-high. Cook 8 to 10 minutes, stirring occasionally, until ravioli are tender.

1 Serving: Calories 495 (Calories from Fat 270); Total Fat 30g (Saturated Fat 9g); Cholesterol 135mg; Sodium 620mg; Total Carbohydrate 18g (Dietary Fiber 3g); Protein 38g

Warm Italian peasant bread and herb butter is a delicious combination with this one-dish stew. End the meal on a light note with vanilla frozen yogurt, cappuccino and chocolate-dipped biscotti.

Old-Time Beef and Vegetable Stew

Prep Time: 20 min ▪ Start to Finish: 20 min ▪ 6 Servings

1 lb boneless beef sirloin steak, cut into ½-inch cubes
1 bag (1 lb) frozen stew vegetables, thawed and drained
1 can (15 oz) chunky tomato sauce with garlic and herbs
1 can (14 oz) beef broth
2 cans (5.5 oz each) spicy eight-vegetable juice

1 Spray 12-inch nonstick skillet with cooking spray; heat over medium-high heat. Cook beef in skillet 6 to 8 minutes, stirring occasionally, until brown.

2 Stir in remaining ingredients. Heat to boiling; reduce heat. Cover and simmer 5 minutes, stirring occasionally.

1 Serving: Calories 165 (Calories from Fat 25); Total Fat 3g (Saturated Fat 1g); Cholesterol 40mg; Sodium 920mg; Total Carbohydrate 15g (Dietary Fiber 3g); Protein 19g

"Speedy stew," an oxymoron? Not if you use a tender cut of beef, cube the meat the night before and use ingredients already in your freezer and pantry.

Savory Beef Stew

Prep Time: 15 min ■ Start to Finish: 3 hr 45 min ■ 6 Servings

1½ lb beef stew meat
1 medium onion, cut into 8 wedges
1 can (14.5 oz) stewed tomatoes, undrained
1½ teaspoons seasoned salt
½ teaspoon pepper
1 dried bay leaf
2 cups water
2 tablespoons all-purpose flour
12 small red potatoes (1½ lb), cut in half
1 bag (8 oz) ready-to-eat baby-cut carrots (about 30)

1 Heat oven to 325°F. In ovenproof 4-quart Dutch oven, mix beef, onion, tomatoes, seasoned salt, pepper and bay leaf. In small bowl, mix water and flour; stir into beef mixture.

2 Cover and bake 2 hours, stirring once.

3 Stir in potatoes and carrots. Cover and bake 1 hour to 1 hour 30 minutes longer or until beef and vegetables are tender. Remove bay leaf.

1 Serving: Calories 350 (Calories from Fat 120); Total Fat 13g (Saturated Fat 5g); Cholesterol 70mg; Sodium 610mg; Total Carbohydrate 33g (Dietary Fiber 5g); Protein 26g

Add a bit of rich flavor, if you have the time, by browning the beef in a little oil before assembling the stew.

Continental Pork Stew

Prep Time: 1 hr 10 min ▪ Start to Finish: 1 hr 10 min ▪ 6 Servings

1 tablespoon olive or vegetable oil
1 tablespoon butter or margarine
2 teaspoons finely chopped garlic
1 package (8 oz) sliced fresh
    mushrooms
1½ lb boneless pork loin roast, cut
    into 1-inch pieces
2½ cups chicken broth
1 cup white wine or chicken broth
1½ cups frozen pearl onions

3 medium carrots, cut lengthwise in
    half, then cut into ¼-inch slices
1 small onion studded with 4 whole
    cloves
1 teaspoon salt
⅛ teaspoon pepper
1 cup whipping cream
⅓ cup quick-mixing flour
Chopped fresh parsley, if desired

1 In 4½- to 5-quart Dutch oven, heat oil and butter over medium-high heat. Cook garlic and mushrooms in oil mixture 5 to 6 minutes, stirring frequently, until mushrooms are softened.

2 Stir in pork. Cook 6 to 7 minutes, stirring frequently, until pork is lightly browned.

3 Stir in broth, wine, pearl onions, carrots, onion with cloves, salt and pepper. Heat to boiling; reduce heat to medium-low. Cover and cook 25 to 30 minutes, stirring occasionally, until pork is tender and no longer pink in center.

4 Remove onion with cloves; discard. Beat in whipping cream and flour with wire whisk. Cook 5 to 6 minutes, stirring constantly, until hot and slightly thickened. Sprinkle with parsley.

1 Serving: Calories 450 (Calories from Fat 270); Total Fat 30g (Saturated Fat 13g); Cholesterol 120mg; Sodium 910mg; Total Carbohydrate 15g (Dietary Fiber 2g); Protein 31g

To make the studded onion for the stew, peel the onion, then gently push four whole cloves into it.

Zesty Autumn Pork Stew

Prep Time: 25 min ■ Start to Finish: 25 min ■ 4 Servings

1 lb pork tenderloin, cut into 1-inch cubes
2 medium dark-orange sweet potatoes, peeled, cubed (2 cups)
1 medium green bell pepper, chopped (1 cup)
2 cloves garlic, finely chopped
1 cup coleslaw mix (shredded cabbage and carrots)
1 teaspoon Cajun seasoning
1 can (14 oz) chicken broth

1 Spray 4-quart Dutch oven with cooking spray; heat over medium-high heat. Cook pork in Dutch oven, stirring occasionally, until brown.

2 Stir in remaining ingredients. Heat to boiling; reduce heat. Cover; simmer about 15 minutes, stirring once, until sweet potatoes are tender.

1 Serving: Calories 240 (Calories from Fat 45); Total Fat 5g (Saturated Fat 2g); Cholesterol 70mg; Sodium 640mg; Total Carbohydrate 18g (Dietary Fiber 3g); Protein 30g

Canned vacuum-packed sweet potatoes, cubed, can be substituted for the fresh sweet potatoes. Add them after you reduce the heat in step two, and remember to stir the mixture gently because canned sweet potatoes are very soft and tender.

Quick Jambalaya

Prep Time: 30 min ▪ Start to Finish: 30 min ▪ 4 Servings

1 package (7 to 8 oz) frozen brown-and-serve sausage links
1½ cups uncooked instant rice
1½ cups chicken broth
1 teaspoon chopped fresh or ¼ teaspoon dried thyme leaves
¼ teaspoon chili powder
⅛ teaspoon ground red pepper (cayenne)
1 small green bell pepper, chopped (½ cup)
1 small onion, chopped (¼ cup)
1 can (14.5 oz) stewed tomatoes, undrained
1 package (10 oz) frozen quick-cooking cleaned shrimp

1 Cut sausages diagonally into 1-inch slices. In deep 10-inch skillet, cook as directed on package; drain.

2 Stir in remaining ingredients. Heat to boiling, stirring occasionally; reduce heat. Simmer uncovered 10 minutes, stirring occasionally.

1 Serving: Calories 500 (Calories from Fat 200); Total Fat 22g (Saturated Fat 8g); Cholesterol 190mg; Sodium 1360mg; Total Carbohydrate 45g (Dietary Fiber 2g); Protein 30g

Cut fat and calories! Omit sausage links to reduce the fat to 2 grams and the calories to 280.

Shrimp Gumbo

Prep Time: 1 hr 20 min ▮ Start to Finish: 1 hr 20 min ▮ 6 Servings

¼ cup butter or margarine
2 medium onions, sliced
1 medium green bell pepper, cut into
    thin strips
2 cloves garlic, finely chopped
2 tablespoons all-purpose flour
3 cups beef broth
½ teaspoon red pepper sauce
¼ teaspoon salt
¼ teaspoon pepper
1 dried bay leaf

1 box (10 oz) frozen cut okra,
    thawed, drained
1 can (14.5 oz) whole tomatoes,
    undrained
1 can (6 oz) tomato paste
1 lb uncooked deveined peeled
    medium shrimp, thawed if
    frozen, tail shells removed
3 cups hot cooked rice
¼ cup chopped fresh parsley

1 In 4-quart Dutch oven, melt butter over medium heat. Cook onions, bell pepper and garlic in butter 5 minutes, stirring occasionally. Stir in flour. Cook over medium heat, stirring constantly, until bubbly; remove from heat.

2 Stir in remaining ingredients except shrimp, rice and parsley, breaking up tomatoes. Heat to boiling; reduce heat to low. Simmer uncovered 45 minutes, stirring occasionally.

3 Stir shrimp into gumbo. Cover and simmer about 5 minutes or until shrimp are pink and firm. Remove bay leaf. Serve soup in bowls over rice. Sprinkle with parsley.

1 Serving: Calories 295 (Calories from Fat 80); Total Fat 9g (Saturated Fat 5g); Cholesterol 125mg; Sodium 1120mg; Total Carbohydrate 40g (Dietary Fiber 5g); Protein 19g

Italian Seafood Stew with Garlic-Herb Croutons

Prep Time: 1 hr ▪ Start to Finish: 1 hr 30 min ▪ 8 Servings

12 fresh clams in shells

2 tablespoons white vinegar

12 fresh mussels in shells

2 bottles (8 oz each) clam juice

2 cans (14.5 oz each) diced tomatoes, undrained

2 cans (15 oz each) tomato sauce

1 cup dry white wine or water

1 container (7 oz) refrigerated pesto

1 lb cod fillets, cut into bite-size pieces

½ lb uncooked deveined peeled medium shrimp (about 16), thawed if frozen, tail shells removed

½ lb uncooked sea scallops (about 16), thawed if frozen

3 tablespoons butter or margarine, softened

16 slices (½ inch thick) French bread

1 Discard any broken-shell or open (dead) clams. In large container, place remaining clams. Cover with 1½ cups water and the vinegar. Let stand 30 minutes; drain. Scrub clams in cold water.

2 Meanwhile, discard any broken-shell or open (dead) mussels. Scrub remaining mussels in cold water, removing any barnacles with a dull paring knife. Pull beard by giving it a tug (using a kitchen towel may help). If you have trouble removing it, use a pliers to grip and pull gently. Place mussels in large container. Cover with cool water. Agitate water with hand, then drain and discard water. Repeat several times until water runs clear; drain.

3 Heat oven to 350°F. In 4-quart Dutch oven, mix clam juice, tomatoes, tomato sauce, wine and ½ cup of the pesto. Layer cod, shrimp, scallops, mussels and clams in Dutch oven. Heat to boiling over medium-high heat; reduce heat. Cover; simmer 15 to 20 minutes or until mussel and clam shells have opened.

4 Meanwhile, in small bowl, mix butter and remaining pesto until well blended. Spread on both sides of bread. On ungreased cookie sheet, place bread in single layer. Bake 10 to 15 minutes, turning once, until toasted on both sides.

5 Discard any mussels or clams that don't open. Spoon stew into soup bowls; top with croutons.

1 Serving: Calories 450 (Calories from Fat 190); Total Fat 21g (Saturated Fat 5g); Cholesterol 110mg; Sodium 1590mg; Total Carbohydrate 33g (Dietary Fiber 4g); Protein 32g

Have all the ingredients assembled on a tray or cookie sheet in your refrigerator so you can whip this up in minutes.

Bean and Vegetable Stew with Polenta

Prep Time: 1 hr 15 min ▪ Start to Finish: 1 hr 15 min ▪ 4 Servings

1 tablespoon olive or vegetable oil
1 medium onion, coarsely chopped (½ cup)
1 medium yellow or green bell pepper, coarsely chopped (1 cup)
2 teaspoons finely chopped garlic
2 medium carrots, cut into ¼-inch slices (1 cup)
2 cans (14.5 oz each) diced tomatoes with basil, undrained

1 can (15 to 16 oz) black-eyed peas, rinsed, drained
1 can (19 oz) cannellini (white kidney) beans, rinsed, drained
1 cup water
1 teaspoon Italian seasoning
½ teaspoon salt
¼ teaspoon pepper
1 roll (16 oz) refrigerated polenta
1 cup frozen cut green beans (from 1-lb bag)

1 In 4½- to 5-quart Dutch oven, heat oil over medium heat. Cook onion, bell pepper and garlic in oil 5 to 6 minutes, stirring frequently, until onion is softened.

2 Stir in remaining ingredients except polenta and green beans. Heat to boiling; reduce heat to medium-low. Cover and cook 35 to 40 minutes, stirring occasionally, until carrots are tender and stew is hot. Meanwhile, cook polenta as directed on package; keep warm.

3 Stir frozen green beans into stew. Cover and cook 5 to 6 minutes, stirring occasionally, until beans are hot. To serve, spoon stew over polenta.

1 Serving: Calories 440 (Calories from Fat 45); Total Fat 5g (Saturated Fat 1g); Cholesterol 0mg; Sodium 1140mg; Total Carbohydrate 91g (Dietary Fiber 20g); Protein 27g

Call your friends, and treat them to this Italian-style stew. Toss together a Caesar salad, pick up some rolls from your favorite bakery and share great conversation over a glass of red wine.

Indian Lentil Stew

Prep Time: 55 min ▮ Start to Finish: 55 min ▮ 4 Servings

2 tablespoons butter or margarine
1 large onion, chopped (1 cup)
1 tablespoon curry powder
2 tablespoons all-purpose flour
1 can (14 oz) vegetable broth
¾ cup dried lentils (6 oz), sorted, rinsed
½ teaspoon salt
½ cup apple juice
3 cups pieces (1 inch) peeled dark-orange sweet potatoes
1 cup frozen sweet peas (from 1-lb bag)
Sour cream or plain yogurt, if desired
Chutney, if desired

1 In 3-quart saucepan, melt butter over medium-high heat. Add onion and curry powder; cook 2 minutes, stirring occasionally. Stir in flour. Gradually add broth, stirring constantly, until thickened.

2 Stir in lentils and salt. Reduce heat to low; cover and simmer 20 minutes, stirring occasionally.

3 Stir in apple juice, sweet potatoes and peas. Heat to boiling. Reduce heat to low; cover and simmer 15 to 20 minutes, stirring occasionally, until vegetables are tender. Top individual servings with sour cream and chutney.

1 Serving: Calories 360 (Calories from Fat 60); Total Fat 7g (Saturated Fat 3g); Cholesterol 15mg; Sodium 790mg; Total Carbohydrate 62g (Dietary Fiber 12g); Protein 14g

Curry powder is made of many flavors, most often including cardamom, chiles, cinnamon, fennel seed, fenugreek, cumin, turmeric, nutmeg, coriander and cloves. The apple juice in this easy stew adds just a touch of sweetness and enhances the curry.

Cajun Barley Stew

Prep Time: 15 min ▪ Start to Finish: 35 min ▪ 4 Servings

2 teaspoons vegetable oil
1 large onion, chopped (1 cup)
1 medium stalk celery, chopped (½ cup)
½ cup uncooked quick-cooking barley
5 cups tomato juice
1 to 2 teaspoons Cajun or Creole seasoning
2 cans (15.5 oz each) great northern or navy beans, drained, rinsed
¼ cup chopped fresh parsley

1 In 12-inch skillet, heat oil over medium-high heat. Add onion and celery; cook, stirring occasionally, until crisp-tender.

2 Stir in remaining ingredients except parsley. Heat to boiling. Reduce heat to low; cover and simmer about 20 minutes or until barley is tender. Stir in parsley and serve.

1 Serving: Calories 460 (Calories from Fat 30); Total Fat 4g (Saturated Fat 1g); Cholesterol 0mg; Sodium 1260mg; Total Carbohydrate 83g (Dietary Fiber 18g); Protein 23g

Quick-cooking barley is a super time-saver! It cooks in less than half the time of regular barley. If Cajun or Creole seasoning isn't available, use two teaspoons chili powder, ½ teaspoon salt and ¼ teaspoon pepper.

Baked "Veggie Burger" Stew

Prep Time: 15 min ▪ Start to Finish: 1 hr 15 min ▪ 4 Servings

2 medium potatoes, cubed (2 cups)
2 small turnips, peeled, cubed
½ medium rutabaga, peeled, cubed
    (2 cups)
2 medium stalks celery, sliced (1 cup)
2 medium carrots, sliced (1 cup)
3 small onions, cut into fourths
½ cup all-purpose flour
2 cups vegetable or beef broth
1 can (14.5 oz) whole tomatoes,
    undrained

2 tablespoons chopped fresh or ¾
    teaspoon dried thyme leaves
2 tablespoons chopped fresh or
    ¾ teaspoon dried marjoram
    leaves
¼ teaspoon salt
¼ teaspoon pepper
1 bay leaf
4 frozen vegetarian burgers, thawed,
    cut into 1-inch pieces

1 Heat oven to 350°F. In ovenproof 4-quart Dutch oven, mix potatoes, turnips, rutabaga, celery, carrots and onions.

2 In medium bowl, mix flour and broth until smooth. Stir broth mixture and remaining ingredients except burger pieces into vegetable mixture, breaking up tomatoes. Heat to boiling over medium-high heat. Stir in burger pieces.

3 Cover and bake 50 to 60 minutes, stirring occasionally, until vegetables are tender. Remove bay leaf.

1 Serving: Calories 300 (Calories from Fat 35); Total Fat 4g (Saturated Fat 1g); Cholesterol 0mg; Sodium 1250mg; Total Carbohydrate 55g (Dietary Fiber 9g); Protein 18g

Thick and hearty stews offer those with robust appetites something to sink their teeth into, and this recipe fills the bill! Complete the meal with a tossed salad and crusty bread. Warm a double-crust fruit pie in the oven for dessert.

Garden Vegetable Stew

Prep Time: 10 min ▪ Start to Finish: 45 min ▪ 12 Servings

¼ cup butter or margarine

3 medium onions, chopped (1½ cups)

4 medium carrots, thinly sliced (2 cups)

4 cans (14 oz each) vegetable broth

1⅓ cups uncooked brown or regular long-grain rice

2 cups frozen whole kernel corn

2 tablespoons chopped fresh basil leaves or 2 teaspoons dried basil leaves

2 teaspoons chopped fresh thyme leaves or ½ teaspoon dried thyme leaves

½ teaspoon pepper

8 new potatoes, cut into fourths

2 large bell peppers, cut into 2×½-inch strips

2 medium zucchini, thinly sliced (4 cups)

1 In 6-quart Dutch oven, melt butter over medium heat. Cook onions and carrots in butter, stirring occasionally, until onions are tender.

2 Stir in broth and rice. Heat to boiling; reduce heat. Cover and simmer 20 minutes.

3 Stir in remaining ingredients. Cover and simmer 10 to 15 minutes or until vegetables are tender.

1 Serving: Calories 220 (Calories from Fat 45); Total Fat 5g (Saturated Fat 3g); Cholesterol 10mg; Sodium 650mg; Total Carbohydrate 44g (Dietary Fiber 5g); Protein 5g

For a bit more color, use one zucchini and one yellow summer squash, thinly sliced, instead of two zucchini.

Southwestern Stew with Corn Dumplings

Prep Time: 15 min ▌ Start to Finish: 40 min ▌ 4 Servings

1 tablespoon vegetable oil
1 large onion, chopped (1 cup)
2 cups cubed peeled dark-orange sweet potatoes or butternut squash
1 cup frozen whole kernel corn (from 1-lb bag)
1 can (15 to 16 oz) garbanzo beans, drained, rinsed
1 jar (16 oz) chunky-style salsa (2 cups)
1 cup water
¼ teaspoon ground cinnamon
1 pouch (6.5 oz) cornbread & muffin mix
½ cup fat-free (skim) milk
1 tablespoon vegetable oil
1 tablespoon roasted sunflower nuts, if desired

1 Heat oven to 425°F. In ovenproof 4-quart Dutch oven, heat 1 tablespoon oil over medium-high heat. Add onion; cook about 5 minutes, stirring occasionally, until crisp-tender. Stir in sweet potatoes, corn, beans, salsa, water and cinnamon. Heat to boiling, stirring occasionally.

2 In small bowl, mix corn muffin mix, milk and 1 tablespoon oil. Stir in nuts. Drop dough by 8 spoonfuls onto vegetable mixture.

3 Bake uncovered 20 to 25 minutes or until toothpick inserted in center of dumplings comes out clean.

1 Serving: Calories 560 (Calories from Fat 140); Total Fat 15g (Saturated Fat 3g); Cholesterol 0mg; Sodium 1030mg; Total Carbohydrate 90g (Dietary Fiber 15g); Protein 16g

Chili Mole

Chili with Corn Dumplings

Slow Cooker Beef and Bean Chili

Slow Cooker Texas Chuck Wagon Chili

Chipotle Pork Chili

Chicken Enchilada Chili

Buffalo Chicken Chili

Cincinnati Chili

White Bean–Chicken Chili

Three-Bean Chili

Home-Style Vegetable Chili

Chili Verde

Ratatouille Chili

Cheesy Chicken and Ham Chowder

Corn and Shrimp Chowder

New England Clam Chowder

Seafood Chowder

Chunky Vegetable Chowder

Jalapeño-Potato Chowder

Creamy Corn and Broccoli Chowder

4

chilies & chowders

Chili Mole

Prep Time: 15 min ▪ Start to Finish: 4 hr 15 min ▪ 6 Servings

1 lb lean (at least 80%) ground beef
1 medium onion, chopped (½ cup)
1 package (1.25 oz) Tex-Mex chili seasoning mix
1 can (28 oz) diced tomatoes, undrained
1 can (28 oz) crushed tomatoes, undrained
1 can (15 oz) spicy chili beans in sauce, undrained
1 oz unsweetened baking chocolate, coarsely chopped

1 Spray 4- to 5-quart slow cooker with cooking spray. In 10-inch skillet, cook beef and onion over medium heat 8 to 10 minutes, stirring occasionally, until beef is thoroughly cooked; drain.

2 In cooker, mix beef mixture and remaining ingredients.

3 Cover; cook on Low heat setting 4 to 6 hours. Stir well before serving.

1 Serving: Calories 310 (Calories from Fat 110); Total Fat 12g (Saturated Fat 5g); Cholesterol 45mg; Sodium 1100mg; Total Carbohydrate 29g (Dietary Fiber 8g); Protein 20g

Mole (MOH-lay) refers to a Mexican sauce which is characterized by the addition of chocolate. Serve with wedges of warm cornbread and slices of Cheddar cheese.

Chili with Corn Dumplings

Prep Time: 45 min ■ Start to Finish: 1 hr 20 min ■ 6 Servings

Chili

1½ lb ground beef
¾ cup chopped onion
1 can (15.25 oz) whole kernel sweet
   corn, undrained
1 can (14.5 oz) stewed tomatoes,
   undrained
1 can (15 oz) tomato sauce
2 tablespoons chili powder
1 teaspoon red pepper sauce

Corn Dumplings

1⅓ cups Original Bisquick® mix
⅔ cup cornmeal
⅔ cup milk
3 tablespoons chopped fresh
   cilantro
Reserved ½ cup whole kernel corn

1 In 4½- to 5-quart Dutch oven, cook beef and onion over medium-high heat, stirring frequently, until beef is brown; drain.

2 Reserve ½ cup of the corn for dumplings. Stir remaining corn with liquid, the tomatoes, tomato sauce, chili powder and pepper sauce into beef mixture. Heat to boiling; reduce heat to low. Cover and simmer 15 minutes.

3 Meanwhile, in medium bowl, stir together Bisquick mix and cornmeal. Stir in milk, cilantro and corn just until dry ingredients are moistened.

4 Drop dough by rounded tablespoonfuls onto simmering chili. Cover and cook 25 to 30 minutes or until dumplings are firm when pressed.

1 Serving: Calories 515 (Calories from Fat 200); Total Fat 22g (Saturated Fat 8g); Cholesterol 65mg; Sodium 1300mg; Total Carbohydrate 56g (Dietary Fiber 6g); Protein 29g

You can use either white or yellow cornmeal to make the dumplings for this mildly spicy meal-in-a-bowl. Pair with a salad of mixed greens, grapes and toasted walnuts, and dinner is served.

Slow Cooker Beef and Bean Chili

Prep Time: 25 min ▮ Start to Finish: 8 hr 25 min ▮ 5 Servings

1 tablespoon olive or vegetable oil
2 medium onions, coarsely chopped (1 cup)
2 teaspoons finely chopped garlic
2 tablespoons chili powder
1 tablespoon ground cumin
1 teaspoon salt
⅛ teaspoon pepper
2 lb beef stew meat
2 cans (14.5 oz each) diced tomatoes with green chiles, undrained
2 cans (15 oz each) black beans, rinsed, drained
½ cup water

1 In 12-inch skillet, heat oil over medium-high heat. Cook onions and garlic in oil 4 to 5 minutes, stirring frequently, until onions are softened.

2 Stir in chili powder, cumin, salt, pepper and beef. Cook 6 to 8 minutes, stirring occasionally, until beef is lightly browned.

3 Place beef mixture in 3- to 4-quart slow cooker. Stir in tomatoes, beans and water.

4 Cover and cook on Low heat setting 8 to 10 hours. Stir well before serving.

1 Serving: Calories 625 (Calories from Fat 235); Total Fat 26g (Saturated Fat 9g); Cholesterol 110mg; Sodium 1660mg; Total Carbohydrate 58g (Dietary Fiber 15g); Protein 55g

This hearty, home-style chili is great served in Parmesan Bread Bowls (page 102). Try it topped with a dollop of sour cream or shredded Cheddar cheese if you like.

Bring on the Bread!

Parmesan Bread Bowls

Prep Time: 15 min
Start to Finish: 45 min
6 Bread Bowls

These versatile bowls make great containers for thick stews, creamed meat, vegetable mixtures or even savory salads.

1 package regular or quick active dry yeast
¼ cup warm water (105°F to 115°F)
2 tablespoons sugar
3 cups all-purpose flour
3 teaspoons baking powder
¾ teaspoon salt
⅓ cup grated Parmesan cheese
¼ cup shortening
1 cup buttermilk

1   In small bowl, dissolve yeast in warm water. Stir in sugar; set aside.

2   In large bowl, mix flour, baking powder, salt and cheese. Cut in shortening, using pastry blender or crisscrossing 2 knives, until mixture looks like fine crumbs. Stir in yeast mixture and just enough buttermilk so dough leaves side of bowl and forms a ball.

3   Place dough on lightly floured surface. Knead about 1 minute or until smooth. Cover and let rise in warm place 10 minutes.

4   Heat oven to 375°F. Grease outsides of six 10-ounce custard cups. In ungreased 15×10-inch pan, place cups upside down. Divide dough into 6 equal parts. Pat or roll each part into 7-inch circle. Shape dough circles over outsides of custard cups. (Do not allow to curl under edges of cups.)

5   Bake 18 to 22 minutes or until golden brown. Carefully lift bread bowls from custard cups; bread will be hot. Cool bread bowls upright on wire cooling rack.

Bowled Over

Instead of serving soup, stew or chili in soup bowls, bowl them over by serving it in a fun, new way:

- Extra-large coffee mugs
- Hollowed-out hard rolls or kaiser rolls, leaving ¼-inch thick shell (best for very thick mixtures)
- Hollowed-out pumpkin for whole recipe or baby pumpkins for individual servings
- Line individual serving bowls with flour tortillas
- Mini casserole or gratin dishes
- Soup plates

Cheese-Garlic Biscuits

Prep Time: 5 min
Start to Finish: 15 min
9 Biscuits

2 cups Original Bisquick mix
⅔ cup milk
½ cup shredded Cheddar cheese
    (2 oz)
2 tablespoons butter or margarine,
    melted
⅛ teaspoon garlic powder

1   Heat oven to 450°F.

2   In medium bowl, stir Bisquick mix, milk and cheese until soft dough forms. Onto ungreased cookie sheet, drop dough by 9 spoonfuls.

3   Bake 8 to 10 minutes or until golden brown. In small bowl, stir together butter and garlic powder; brush over warm biscuits.

Do you have 15 minutes to spare? Surprise your family by baking a batch of these restaurant-style biscuits to serve with your favorite soup, stew or chili!

Bacon Cornbread

Prep Time: 15 min
Start to Finish: 45 min
12 Servings

1½ cups yellow cornmeal
½ cup all-purpose flour
¼ cup vegetable oil or shortening
1½ cups buttermilk
4 slices bacon, crisply cooked and
    crumbled
2 teaspoons baking powder
1 teaspoon sugar
½ teaspoon salt
½ teaspoon baking soda
2 eggs

1   Heat oven to 450°F. Grease 9-inch round or 8-inch square pan.

2   In large bowl, stir together all ingredients; beat vigorously 30 seconds. Pour into pan.

3   Bake 25 to 30 minutes or until golden brown. Serve warm.

Come and get it! Bacon flavors this true Southern-style buttermilk cornbread. It's perfect for soups and stews and to complete Southern-cooked meals.

Slow Cooker Texas Chuck Wagon Chili

Prep Time: 40 min ▪ Start to Finish: 8 hr 40 min ▪ 8 Servings

2 tablespoons olive or vegetable oil
4 large onions, cut into eighths
4 to 4½ lb fresh beef brisket (not corned beef), trimmed of fat and
    cut into 1-inch pieces
1½ tablespoons finely chopped garlic
2½ teaspoons salt
½ teaspoon pepper
2 to 4 dried ancho chiles, coarsely chopped
2 tablespoons ground cumin
3 cups beef broth
2 large yellow, red or green bell peppers, cut into 2½-inch strips
Shredded Cheddar cheese, if desired

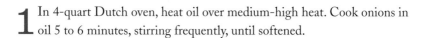

1 In 4-quart Dutch oven, heat oil over medium-high heat. Cook onions in oil 5 to 6 minutes, stirring frequently, until softened.

2 Stir in beef, garlic, salt and pepper. Cook about 13 minutes, stirring occasionally, until beef is lightly browned; drain. In 6-quart slow cooker, place beef mixture. Stir in chiles, cumin and broth.

3 Cover and cook on Low heat setting 8 to 9 hours.

4 Stir in bell peppers. Increase heat setting to High. Cover and cook 10 to 12 minutes or until bell peppers are hot. Serve with cheese.

1 Serving: Calories 435 (Calories from Fat 180); Total Fat 20g (Saturated Fat 7g); Cholesterol 130mg; Sodium 1250mg; Total Carbohydrate 12g (Dietary Fiber 2g); Protein 52g

For a delicious Tex-Mex dinner, serve cornbread and your favorite deli coleslaw.

Chipotle Pork Chili

Prep Time: 1 hr 10 min ■ Start to Finish: 1 hr 10 min ■ 5 Servings

1 tablespoon olive or vegetable oil
2 medium onions, cut in half, then cut into ¼-inch slices and slices separated
2 teaspoons finely chopped garlic
1 teaspoon salt
1 tablespoon ground cumin
⅛ teaspoon pepper
2 lb boneless pork loin roast, cut into 1-inch pieces
1 chipotle chili in adobo sauce, finely chopped, plus 1 teaspoon adobo sauce
    (from 7- to 11-oz can)
3 cans (14.5 oz each) diced tomatoes with green chiles, undrained

1 In 4½- to 5-quart Dutch oven, heat oil over medium-high heat. Cook onions and garlic in oil 4 to 5 minutes, stirring occasionally, until onions are softened.

2 Stir in salt, cumin, pepper and pork. Cook 6 to 8 minutes, stirring frequently, until pork is lightly browned.

3 Stir in chipotle chili, adobo sauce and tomatoes. Heat to boiling; reduce heat to medium-low. Cover and cook 35 to 40 minutes, stirring occasionally, until pork is no longer pink in center.

1 Serving: Calories 400 (Calories from Fat 160); Total Fat 18g (Saturated Fat 5g); Cholesterol 115mg; Sodium 1300mg; Total Carbohydrate 16g (Dietary Fiber 4g); Protein 43g

Warm flour tortillas make great dippers for this rich, smoky chili. A fresh vegetable plate of carrot, jicama and cucumber sticks and a creamy dip make a cooling side dish.

Chicken Enchilada Chili

Prep Time: 10 min ▮ Start to Finish: 7 hr 10 min ▮ 6 Servings

1¼ lb boneless skinless chicken thighs
1 medium onion, chopped (½ cup)
1 medium yellow or green bell pepper, chopped (1 cup)
2 cans (14.5 oz each) stewed tomatoes with garlic and onion, undrained
2 cans (15 to 16 oz each) chili beans in sauce, undrained
1 can (10 oz) enchilada sauce
⅓ cup sour cream
2 tablespoons chopped fresh cilantro

1 Spray 4- to 5-quart slow cooker with cooking spray. In cooker, mix all ingredients except sour cream and cilantro.

2 Cover and cook on Low heat setting 7 to 8 hours.

3 Stir mixture to break up chicken. Top each serving with sour cream and cilantro.

1 Serving: Calories 340 (Calories from Fat 100); Total Fat 11g (Saturated Fat 4g); Cholesterol 65mg; Sodium 1700mg; Total Carbohydrate 38g (Dietary Fiber 8g); Protein 30g

For super-quick dinners and totable lunches, freeze the chili in single-serving freezer containers. Thaw, then heat in the microwave on High for 4 to 5 minutes, stirring once or twice, until hot.

Buffalo Chicken Chili

Prep Time: 45 min ▪ Start to Finish: 45 min ▪ 6 Servings

1 tablespoon vegetable oil
1 large onion, chopped (1 cup)
1 medium red or yellow bell pepper, chopped (1 cup)
2 cups cubed deli rotisserie chicken (from 2- to 2½-lb chicken)
1 cup chicken broth
1 tablespoon chili powder
5 or 6 drops red pepper sauce
2 cans (15 to 16 oz each) pinto beans, drained
1 can (28 oz) crushed tomatoes, undrained
1 can (14.5 oz) diced tomatoes, undrained
½ cup sliced celery
½ cup crumbled blue cheese

1 In 3-quart saucepan, heat oil over medium-high heat. Cook onion and bell pepper in oil about 5 minutes, stirring occasionally, until crisp-tender.

2 Stir in remaining ingredients except celery and blue cheese. Heat to boiling; reduce heat to medium-low. Simmer uncovered 10 to 15 minutes, stirring occasionally. Serve topped with celery and blue cheese.

1 Serving: Calories 380 (Calories from Fat 90); Total Fat 10g (Saturated Fat 4g); Cholesterol 50mg; Sodium 1060mg; Total Carbohydrate 43g (Dietary Fiber 13g); Protein 28g

Serve the chili over hot cooked spaghetti for Cincinnati-Style Buffalo Spaghetti. Keep the bottle of red pepper sauce handy for those who like their chili hot.

Cincinnati Chili

Prep Time: 30 min ■ Start to Finish: 30 min ■ 5 Servings

10 oz uncooked spaghetti
1 tablespoon vegetable oil
1 lb ground turkey breast
1 medium onion, chopped (½ cup)
1 clove garlic, finely chopped
1 jar (26 to 28 oz) chunky vegetable-style tomato pasta sauce
1 can (15 to 16 oz) kidney beans, rinsed, drained
2 tablespoons chili powder

1 Cook and drain spaghetti as directed on package.

2 While spaghetti is cooking, in 10-inch skillet, heat oil over medium heat. Cook turkey, onion and garlic in oil 5 to 6 minutes, stirring occasionally, until turkey is no longer pink.

3 Stir pasta sauce, beans and chili powder into turkey mixture; reduce heat to low. Simmer uncovered 10 minutes, stirring occasionally. Serve chili over spaghetti.

1 Serving: Calories 625 (Calories from Fat 135); Total Fat 15g (Saturated Fat 3g); Cholesterol 60mg; Sodium 1020mg; Total Carbohydrate 96g (Dietary Fiber 11g); Protein 37g

Have ground beef in the freezer? You can use it instead of the turkey, and you won't need the oil.

White Bean–Chicken Chili

Prep Time: 20 min ▪ Start to Finish: 20 min ▪ 6 Servings

2 tablespoons butter or margarine
1 large onion, coarsely chopped (1 cup)
2 cloves garlic, finely chopped
3 cups cubed deli rotisserie chicken (from 2- to 2½-lb chicken)
½ teaspoon ground cumin
2 cans (10 oz each) diced tomatoes with green chiles, undrained
1 can (15.5 oz) great northern beans, drained, rinsed
Sour cream, if desired
Chopped fresh cilantro, if desired

1 In 4½- to 5-quart Dutch oven, melt butter over medium-high heat. Cook onion and garlic in butter, stirring occasionally, until onion is tender.

2 Stir in remaining ingredients except sour cream and cilantro. Heat to boiling; reduce heat to low. Simmer uncovered 2 to 3 minutes, stirring occasionally, until hot.

3 Top each serving with sour cream; sprinkle with cilantro.

1 Serving: Calories 280 (Calories from Fat 80); Total Fat 9g (Saturated Fat 4g); Cholesterol 70mg; Sodium 650mg; Total Carbohydrate 23g (Dietary Fiber 6g); Protein 27g

Instead of crackers, serve this chili with tortilla chips for a little crunch.

Three-Bean Chili

Prep Time: 45 min ▪ Start to Finish: 45 min ▪ 4 Servings

1 can (14 oz) vegetable or chicken broth
1 large onion, chopped (1 cup)
2 cloves garlic, finely chopped
2 medium tomatoes, cut into ½-inch pieces (2 cups)
1 tablespoon chopped fresh or 1 teaspoon dried oregano leaves
2½ teaspoons chili powder
1 can (15 to 16 oz) chili beans in sauce, undrained
1 can (15 oz) dark red kidney beans, drained
1 can (15 oz) garbanzo beans, drained
2 tablespoons chopped fresh cilantro or parsley

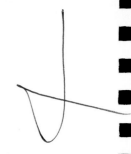

1 In 4-quart Dutch oven, heat ¼ cup of the broth to boiling over medium-high heat. Cook onion and garlic in broth about 5 minutes, stirring occasionally, until onion is tender.

2 Stir in remaining broth, tomatoes, oregano and chili powder. Heat to boiling; reduce heat to low. Cover; simmer 15 minutes, stirring occasionally.

3 Stir in chili, kidney and garbanzo beans. Heat to boiling; reduce heat to low. Simmer uncovered 10 minutes, stirring occasionally. Sprinkle with cilantro.

1 Serving: Calories 420 (Calories from Fat 35); Total Fat 4g (Saturated Fat 0g); Cholesterol 0mg; Sodium 1580mg; Total Carbohydrate 73g (Dietary Fiber 19g); Protein 23g

You can substitute beans as you like for this chili. For an interesting change of flavor, why not try black beans instead of the kidney or garbanzo beans?

Home-Style Vegetable Chili

Prep Time: 40 min ■ Start to Finish: 40 min ■ 6 Servings

2 tablespoons vegetable oil
1 large onion, chopped (1 cup)
1 medium green bell pepper, chopped (1 cup)
2 medium carrots, chopped (1 cup)
1 pasilla chile, seeded, chopped (¾ cup), or 1 can (4.5 oz) chopped green chiles
1 cup water
1 tablespoon chili powder
1 teaspoon ground cumin
¾ teaspoon salt
2 cans (15 to 16 oz each) red kidney beans, drained, rinsed
2 cans (14.5 oz each) diced tomatoes, undrained
Shredded Cheddar cheese, if desired

1 In 3-quart saucepan, heat oil over medium-high heat. Add onion, bell pepper, carrots and chile; cook 3 to 5 minutes, stirring occasionally until crisp-tender.

2 Stir in remaining ingredients except cheese. Heat to boiling. Reduce heat to medium-low; simmer uncovered 10 to 15 minutes, stirring occasionally, until vegetables are tender. Sprinkle individual servings with cheese.

1 Serving: Calories 280 (Calories from Fat 50); Total Fat 6g (Saturated Fat 1g); Cholesterol 0mg; Sodium 520mg; Total Carbohydrate 43g (Dietary Fiber 11g); Protein 13g

Pasilla chiles, 6 to 8 inches long, are medium-hot in flavor. When fresh, they are sometimes referred to as chilaca chiles. Canned green chiles can be substituted, but the flavor may be slightly milder.

Chili Verde

Prep Time: 45 min ▪ Start to Finish: 45 min ▪ 4 Servings

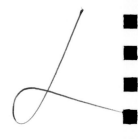

2 small zucchini, cut into ½-inch pieces (2 cups)
1 large green bell pepper, cut into ½-inch pieces (1½ cups)
½ lb small red potatoes, cut into ½-inch pieces (1½ cups)
2½ cups water
½ cup salsa verde (from 12- to 16-oz jar)
1 can (15.5 oz) white or yellow hominy, drained, rinsed
1 extra-large vegetarian vegetable bouillon cube
2 teaspoons chili powder
¼ cup sour cream

1 In 3-quart saucepan, mix all ingredients except sour cream. Heat to boiling over high heat. Reduce heat to low; cover and simmer 15 to 18 minutes, stirring occasionally, until potatoes are tender.

2 Top individual servings with 1 tablespoon sour cream.

1 Serving: Calories 200 (Calories from Fat 40); Total Fat 5g (Saturated Fat 2g); Cholesterol 10mg; Sodium 940mg; Total Carbohydrate 35g (Dietary Fiber 7g); Protein 5g

Salsa verde means "green salsa" that's made with tomatillos and green chiles, versus those made strictly with jalapeños.

Ratatouille Chili

Prep Time: 25 min ■ Start to Finish: 25 min ■ 4 Servings

2 tablespoons olive or vegetable oil
1 large eggplant (1 lb), cut into ½-inch cubes (4 cups)
1 large onion, chopped (1 cup)
1 medium green bell pepper, chopped (1 cup)
1 clove garlic, finely chopped
½ cup sliced zucchini
3 teaspoons chili powder
1 teaspoon chopped fresh or ¼ teaspoon dried basil leaves
¼ teaspoon salt
1 can (15.5 oz) great northern beans, drained, rinsed
1 can (14.5 oz) whole tomatoes, undrained
1 can (8 oz) tomato sauce

1 In 4-quart Dutch oven, heat oil over medium-high heat. Add eggplant, onion, bell pepper and garlic; cook, stirring occasionally, until vegetables are crisp-tender.

2 Stir in remaining ingredients, breaking up tomatoes. Cook about 10 minutes, stirring occasionally, until zucchini is tender.

1 Serving: Calories 300 (Calories from Fat 70); Total Fat 8g (Saturated Fat 1g); Cholesterol 0mg; Sodium 670mg; Total Carbohydrate 45g (Dietary Fiber 12g); Protein 13g

From the Provence region of France, the popular dish of ratatouille is often served as a side dish or appetizer. The flavors typical of this dish include eggplant, zucchini, tomatoes, olive oil and garlic, all of which are found in this savory chili version.

Cheesy Chicken and Ham Chowder

Prep Time: 20 min ▪ Start to Finish: 20 min ▪ 4 Servings

2 cans (18.5 oz each) ready-to-serve russet potatoes and broccoli chowder
1 cup cubed cooked chicken breast
1 cup diced cooked ham
1 cup shredded Cheddar cheese (4 oz)

1 In 3-quart saucepan, heat soup, chicken and ham over medium-high heat 5 minutes, stirring occasionally.

2 Slowly stir in cheese. Cook about 2 minutes, stirring frequently, until cheese is melted.

1 Serving: Calories 410 (Calories from Fat 220); Total Fat 24g (Saturated Fat 10g); Cholesterol 90mg; Sodium 1620mg; Total Carbohydrate 18g (Dietary Fiber 2g); Protein 30g

Leftover chopped rotisserie chicken works well for the cubed chicken breast. Try pairing different meats and cheeses to come up with a delicious new creation every time.

Corn and Shrimp Chowder

Prep Time: 50 min ■ Start to Finish: 50 min ■ 7 Servings

4 slices bacon, cut into ½-inch pieces
1 medium onion, coarsely chopped (½ cup)
1 medium stalk celery, coarsely chopped (½ cup)
6 small red potatoes, cut into ½-inch pieces
2 cups frozen whole kernel corn (from 1-lb bag)
¼ teaspoon dried thyme leaves
4 cups chicken broth
¼ cup quick-mixing flour
2 cups half-and-half
1 package (12 oz) frozen uncooked medium shrimp, peeled, deveined and tails
    removed (do not thaw)
½ teaspoon salt
⅛ teaspoon pepper

1 In 5- to 6-quart Dutch oven, cook bacon over medium-high heat 5 to 6 minutes, stirring frequently, until crisp. Stir in onion, celery, potatoes, frozen corn and thyme. Cook 5 to 6 minutes, stirring frequently, until onion and celery are softened.

2 Beat in broth and flour with wire whisk. Heat to boiling; reduce heat to medium. Cover and boil about 15 minutes, stirring occasionally, until potatoes are tender and soup is slightly thickened.

3 Stir in half-and-half, shrimp, salt and pepper. Cover and cook 5 to 6 minutes, stirring occasionally, until shrimp are pink and firm.

1 Serving: Calories 280 (Calories from Fat 100); Total Fat 11g (Saturated Fat 6g); Cholesterol 100mg; Sodium 930mg; Total Carbohydrate 31g (Dietary Fiber 3g); Protein 16g

Make this cozy soup the star of a simple meal. A basket of hearty whole-grain or sourdough rolls or breadsticks is the only accompaniment needed.

Jalapeño-Potato Chowder

Prep Time: 35 min ■ Start to Finish: 35 min ■ 4 Servings

3 tablespoons butter or margarine
1 medium onion, chopped (½ cup)
1 small green bell pepper, chopped (½ cup)
3 tablespoons all-purpose flour
2½ cups milk
3 cups diced cooked potatoes
1 cup frozen whole kernel corn (from 1-lb bag)
1 to 2 tablespoons fresh or canned chopped jalapeño chiles
¾ teaspoon salt
1 teaspoon fresh or ¼ teaspoon dried thyme leaves
½ cup shredded Swiss cheese (2 oz), if desired

1 In 2-quart saucepan, melt butter over medium heat. Add onion and bell pepper; cook 3 to 5 minutes, stirring occasionally, until crisp-tender.

2 Stir in flour. Gradually add milk, stirring constantly, until mixture is boiling.

3 Stir in remaining ingredients except cheese. Cook 5 to 10 minutes, stirring occasionally, until corn is tender. Serve soup topped with cheese.

1 Serving: Calories 320 (Calories from Fat 110); Total Fat 12g (Saturated Fat 6g); Cholesterol 35mg; Sodium 580mg; Total Carbohydrate 43g (Dietary Fiber 3g); Protein 9g

Next time try Jalapeño-Tuna-Potato Chowder. Omit whole kernel corn. Add one can (6 ounces) white tuna in water, drained, with the remaining ingredients in step three.

Creamy Corn and Broccoli Chowder

Prep Time: 30 min ▪ Start to Finish: 30 min ▪ 6 Servings

2 tablespoons butter or margarine
1 medium onion, chopped (½ cup)
1 clove garlic, finely chopped
3 tablespoons all-purpose flour
½ teaspoon coarse salt (kosher or sea salt)
⅛ teaspoon pepper
3 cups reduced-sodium chicken broth or vegetable broth
1 bag (1 lb) frozen broccoli cuts
2 cups frozen sweet corn (from 1-lb bag)
1 cup half-and-half

1 In 4-quart saucepan, melt butter over medium heat. Cook onion and garlic in butter 2 to 3 minutes, stirring frequently, until tender. Stir in flour, salt and pepper. Cook, stirring constantly, 1 minute.

2 Stir in broth, broccoli and corn. Heat to boiling over high heat. Reduce heat; simmer 5 to 7 minutes, stirring occasionally, until vegetables are tender.

3 Stir in half-and-half. Cook 2 to 3 minutes, stirring occasionally, until hot (do not boil).

1 Serving: Calories 190 (Calories from Fat 80); Total Fat 9g (Saturated Fat 5g); Cholesterol 25mg; Sodium 530mg; Total Carbohydrate 21g (Dietary Fiber 4g); Protein 7g

Just add your favorite crusty bread, sliced cheeses and fresh fruit to complete the meal.

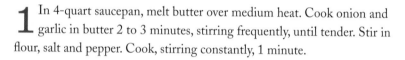

5

slow cooker soups & stews

Hearty Steak and Tater Soup

Prep Time: 20 min ▮ Start to Finish: 8 hr 50 min ▮ 9 Servings

1 lb boneless beef round steak
1 lb small red potatoes, cut into ¼-inch slices (4 cups)
2 medium stalks celery, chopped (1 cup)
2 medium carrots, chopped (1 cup)
1 medium onion, chopped (½ cup)
2 cloves garlic, finely chopped
1 tablespoon beef bouillon granules
½ teaspoon pepper
4 cans (14.5 oz each) beef broth
1 jar (6 oz) sliced mushrooms, undrained
½ cup water
½ cup all-purpose flour

1 Cut beef into 1×¼-inch pieces. In 5-quart slow cooker, mix beef and remaining ingredients except water and flour.

2 Cover and cook on Low heat setting 8 to 9 hours.

3 In small bowl, mix water and flour; gradually stir into soup until blended. Increase heat setting to High. Cover and cook about 30 minutes or until slightly thickened.

1 Serving: Calories 150 (Calories from Fat 20); Total Fat 3g (Saturated Fat 1g); Cholesterol 25mg; Sodium 1340mg; Total Carbohydrate 19g (Dietary Fiber 3g); Protein 15g

Warm sourdough bread, a salad of sliced tomatoes and cucumbers in an herb vinaigrette dressing and glasses of cold apple cider or beer create a stick-to-your-ribs meal.

Beef-Tortellini Soup

Prep Time: 20 min ▪ Start to Finish: 8 hr 50 min ▪ 6 Servings

1 lb beef stew meat
1 large onion, chopped (¾ cup)
1 large carrot, chopped (¾ cup)
1 medium stalk celery, chopped (½ cup)
2 cloves garlic, finely chopped
2 teaspoons sugar
1 can (14.5 oz) diced tomatoes, undrained
2 cans (10.5 oz each) condensed beef consommé
1 teaspoon dried basil leaves
2 cups frozen cheese-filled tortellini
1 cup frozen cut green beans (from 1-lb bag)

1 In 3½- to 4-quart slow cooker, add beef, onion, carrot, celery, garlic, sugar, tomatoes and beef consommé in order listed.

2 Cover; cook on Low heat setting 8 to 9 hours.

3 About 25 minutes before serving, stir in basil, frozen tortellini and green beans. Increase heat setting to High. Cover; cook about 25 minutes or until beans are tender.

1 Serving: Calories 310 (Calories from Fat 120); Total Fat 14g (Saturated Fat 5g); Cholesterol 100mg; Sodium 710mg; Total Carbohydrate 22g (Dietary Fiber 3g); Protein 26g

For a special touch, top each serving with a teaspoon of basil pesto.

Beef and Barley Soup

Prep Time: 20 min ▍ Start to Finish: 9 hr 50 min ▍ 8 Servings

1½ lb beef stew meat
3 medium carrots, sliced (1½ cups)
1 large onion, chopped (1 cup)
2 cloves garlic, finely chopped
⅔ cup frozen whole kernel corn, thawed (from 1-lb bag)
⅔ cup uncooked pearl barley
½ teaspoon salt
½ teaspoon pepper
1 can (14.5 oz) diced tomatoes, undrained
3 cans (14 oz each) beef broth
1 cup frozen sweet peas, thawed (from 1-lb bag)

1 Spray 5- to 6-quart slow cooker with cooking spray. In cooker, mix all ingredients except peas.

2 Cover; cook on Low heat setting 9 to 10 hours.

3 Stir in peas. Increase heat setting to High. Cover; cook 20 to 30 minutes longer or until peas are tender.

1 Serving: Calories 280 (Calories from Fat 100); Total Fat 11g (Saturated Fat 4g); Cholesterol 50mg; Sodium 930mg; Total Carbohydrate 25g (Dietary Fiber 5g); Protein 21g

Pearl barley, which is the most common form, is the perfect grain to cook in the slow cooker. The long, slow cooking produces barley that is tender but not gummy.

Italian Meatball Soup

Prep Time: 10 min ▪ Start to Finish: 8 hr 10 min ▪ 5 Servings

1 bag (16 oz) frozen cooked Italian-style meatballs, thawed
1 can (14 oz) beef broth
1 cup water
1 can (14.5 oz) diced tomatoes with basil, garlic and oregano, undrained
1 can (19 oz) cannellini beans, drained
⅓ cup shredded Parmesan cheese

1 In 3- to 4-quart slow cooker, mix all ingredients except cheese.

2 Cover; cook on Low heat setting 8 to 10 hours.

3 Garnish individual servings with cheese.

1 Serving: Calories 410 (Calories from Fat 140); Total Fat 15g (Saturated Fat 6g); Cholesterol 100mg; Sodium 1540mg; Total Carbohydrate 38g (Dietary Fiber 6g); Protein 31g

Place the package of meatballs in your refrigerator the night before, and they will be thawed in the morning.

Smoked Sausage and Bean Soup

Prep Time: 15 min ▮ Start to Finish: 8 hr 45 min ▮ 7 Servings

1 lb small red potatoes, each cut into 8 pieces (about 3 cups)
4 medium carrots, sliced (2 cups)
1 medium onion, chopped (½ cup)
1 medium stalk celery, sliced (½ cup)
2 cans (15 oz each) navy or cannellini beans, drained, rinsed
2 cans (14 oz each) chicken broth
1 teaspoon dried thyme leaves
½ teaspoon seasoned salt
1 lb fully cooked kielbasa sausage, cut in half lengthwise, then into ¼-inch slices
2 tablespoons chopped fresh parsley

1 Spray 3- to 4-quart slow cooker with cooking spray. In cooker, mix all ingredients except sausage and parsley.

2 Cover; cook on Low heat setting 8 to 9 hours.

3 Stir in sausage and parsley. Cover; cook on Low heat setting 30 minutes longer or until sausage is hot.

1 Serving: Calories 440 (Calories from Fat 170); Total Fat 19g (Saturated Fat 7g); Cholesterol 40mg; Sodium 1220mg; Total Carbohydrate 47g (Dietary Fiber 14g); Protein 20g

If the red potatoes are very small, cut them in half to prevent overcooking. Diced cooked ham can be used in place of the sausage.

Ham and Wild Rice Soup

Prep Time: 15 min ▪ Start to Finish: 7 hr 30 min ▪ 6 Servings

2 cups diced cooked ham
1 cup julienne (matchstick-cut) carrots
¾ cup uncooked wild rice
1 medium onion, chopped (½ cup)
1 can (14 oz) chicken broth
1 can (10.75 oz) reduced-sodium cream of celery soup
¼ teaspoon pepper
3 cups water
1 cup half-and-half
¼ cup sliced almonds
2 tablespoons dry sherry, if desired
¼ cup chopped fresh parsley

1 Spray 3- to 4-quart slow cooker with cooking spray. In cooker, mix all
ingredients except half-and-half, almonds, sherry and parsley.

2 Cover; cook on Low heat setting 7 to 8 hours.

3 Stir in remaining ingredients. Increase heat setting to High. Cover; cook
10 to 15 minutes longer or until hot.

1 Serving: Calories 290 (Calories from Fat 110); Total Fat 12g (Saturated Fat 5g); Cholesterol 40mg;
Sodium 1190mg; Total Carbohydrate 28g (Dietary Fiber 3g); Protein 17g

Look for a bag of julienne-cut carrots or French-cut
cooking carrots in the refrigerated vegetable section of your grocery store.
For best results, we don't recommend using canned or quick-cooking wild
rice for this recipe.

Cheesy Potato Soup

Prep Time: 15 min ▪ Start to Finish: 6 hr 45 min ▪ 6 Servings

1 bag (32 oz) frozen southern-style diced hash brown potatoes, thawed
½ cup frozen chopped onion (from 12-oz bag), thawed
1 medium stalk celery, diced (½ cup)
2 cans (14 oz each) chicken broth
1 cup water
3 tablespoons all-purpose flour
1 cup milk
1 bag (8 oz) shredded American-Cheddar cheese blend (2 cups)
¼ cup real bacon pieces (from 2.8-oz package)
4 medium green onions, sliced (¼ cup)
Pepper, if desired

1 In 3- to 4-quart slow cooker, mix potatoes, onion, celery, broth and water.

2 Cover; cook on Low heat setting 6 to 8 hours.

3 In small bowl, mix flour into milk; stir into potato mixture. Increase heat setting to High. Cover; cook 20 to 30 minutes or until mixture thickens. Stir in cheese until melted. Garnish individual servings with bacon and green onions. Sprinkle with pepper.

1 Serving: Calories 410 (Calories from Fat 140); Total Fat 15g (Saturated Fat 9g); Cholesterol 45mg; Sodium 1210mg; Total Carbohydrate 50g (Dietary Fiber 5g); Protein 19g

Southern-style hash brown potatoes are diced instead of shredded. These work best in this recipe.

Zesty Black Bean Soup

Prep Time: 25 min ▌ Start to Finish: 11 hr 25 min ▌ 9 Servings

2 cups dried black beans (1 lb), sorted, rinsed
10 cups water
8 cups vegetable broth
2 cans (14.5 oz each) diced tomatoes with green chiles, undrained
2 medium carrots, coarsely chopped (1 cup)
2 medium onions, coarsely chopped (1 cup)
¼ cup chopped fresh cilantro
2 teaspoons finely chopped garlic
1 teaspoon salt
¼ teaspoon pepper
⅛ teaspoon ground red pepper (cayenne)
Sour cream, if desired
Chopped fresh cilantro, if desired

1 In 4-quart Dutch oven, heat beans and water to boiling; reduce heat. Simmer uncovered 10 minutes; remove from heat. Cover and let stand 1 hour.

2 Drain beans. In 6-quart slow cooker, place beans and remaining ingredients except sour cream and cilantro.

3 Cover and cook on Low heat setting 10 to 12 hours.

4 Serve soup topped with sour cream and cilantro.

1 Serving: Calories 175 (Calories from Fat 10); Total Fat 1g (Saturated Fat 0g); Cholesterol 0mg; Sodium 1410mg; Total Carbohydrate 40g (Dietary Fiber 8g); Protein 10g

Pinched for time? Soak the beans in cold water overnight rather than using the quick-soak method in the recipe.

Lentil Soup

Prep Time: 15 min ▪ Start to Finish: 8 hr 15 min ▪ 8 Servings

1 lb smoked ham shanks
8 cups chicken broth
1 package (16 oz) dried lentils (2¼ cups), sorted, rinsed
4 medium stalks celery, chopped (2 cups)
4 medium carrots, chopped (2 cups)
3 tablespoons chopped fresh parsley
3 cloves garlic, finely chopped
2 cups shredded fresh spinach

1 In 5- to 6-quart slow cooker, mix all ingredients except spinach.

2 Cover and cook on Low heat setting 8 to 9 hours or until lentils are tender.

3 Remove ham from cooker; place on cutting board. Pull meat from bones, using 2 forks; discard bones and skin. Stir ham and spinach into soup. Stir well before serving.

1 Serving: Calories 205 (Calories from Fat 25); Total Fat 3g (Saturated Fat 1g); Cholesterol 5mg; Sodium 810mg; Total Carbohydrate 37g (Dietary Fiber 14g); Protein 21g

Pair this thick and meaty soup with a crisp green salad tossed with orange segments and a tangy orange vinaigrette.

Split Pea Soup

Prep Time: 15 min ▪ Start to Finish: 8 hr 15 min ▪ 8 Servings

7 cups water
1 package (16 oz) dried split peas (2¼ cups), sorted, rinsed
1 teaspoon salt
¼ teaspoon pepper
3 medium carrots, cut into ¼-inch slices (1½ cups)
2 medium stalks celery, finely chopped (1 cup)
1 medium onion, chopped (½ cup)
1 ham bone, 2 lb ham shanks or 2 lb smoked pork hocks

1 In 4- to 5-quart slow cooker, mix all ingredients except ham. Add ham.

2 Cover and cook on Low heat setting 8 to 10 hours or until peas are tender.

3 Remove ham from cooker; place on cutting board. Pull meat from bones, using 2 forks; discard bones and skin. Stir ham into soup. Stir well before serving.

1 Serving: Calories 175 (Calories from Fat 20); Total Fat 5g (Saturated Fat 1g); Cholesterol 15mg; Sodium 320mg; Total Carbohydrate 34g (Dietary Fiber 12g); Protein 16g

Serve up steaming bowlfuls of this tasty soup with dark rye rolls and a fresh fruit salad.

Hungarian Beef Stew

Prep Time: 10 min ▪ Start to Finish: 7 hr 25 min ▪ 6 Servings

2 lb beef stew meat
6 unpeeled new potatoes, cut into ¾-inch pieces (3 cups)
1 cup frozen small whole onions (from 1-lb bag), thawed
¼ cup all-purpose flour
1 tablespoon paprika
½ teaspoon peppered seasoned salt
¼ teaspoon caraway seed
1 can (14 oz) beef broth
1½ cups frozen sweet peas (from 1-lb bag), thawed
½ cup sour cream

1 Spray 3- to 4-quart slow cooker with cooking spray. In cooker, toss beef, potatoes, onions, flour, paprika, peppered seasoned salt and caraway seed until well mixed. Stir in broth.

2 Cover and cook on Low heat setting 7 to 8 hours.

3 Stir in peas and sour cream. Cover and cook on Low heat setting about 15 minutes or until peas are tender.

1 Serving: Calories 450 (Calories from Fat 200); Total Fat 22g (Saturated Fat 9g); Cholesterol 105mg; Sodium 530mg; Total Carbohydrate 31g (Dietary Fiber 5g); Protein 37g

If you don't have the frozen onions on hand, you can substitute ½ cup chopped onion.

Country French Beef Stew

Prep Time: 25 min ▮ Start to Finish: 7 hr 55 min ▮ 12 Servings

6 slices bacon, cut into ½-inch pieces
1 boneless beef chuck roast (3 lb),
    trimmed of fat, cut into 1-inch
    pieces
1 large onion, cut into ½-inch wedges
3 cups ready-to-serve baby-cut
    carrots
1 cup red Zinfandel wine or
    nonalcoholic red wine
¾ cup beef broth
3 tablespoons all-purpose flour
1 teaspoon dried basil leaves

½ teaspoon dried thyme leaves
½ teaspoon salt
¼ teaspoon pepper
1 can (14.5 oz) diced tomatoes,
    undrained
1 package (8 oz) sliced fresh
    mushrooms (3 cups)
½ cup julienne-cut sun-dried
    tomatoes (not oil-packed)
Hot cooked egg noodles, if desired
Chopped fresh parsley or basil
    leaves, if desired

1 Spray 5- to 6-quart slow cooker with cooking spray. In 12-inch nonstick skillet, cook bacon over medium-high heat, stirring occasionally, until crisp. Place bacon in cooker. Discard all but 1 tablespoon bacon fat in skillet. Cook beef in bacon fat 2 to 3 minutes, stirring occasionally, until brown. Stir onion into beef. Cook 1 minute, stirring occasionally. Spoon mixture into cooker.

2 Stir carrots, wine, broth, flour, basil, thyme, salt, pepper and canned diced tomatoes into mixture in cooker.

3 Cover; cook on Low heat setting 7 to 8 hours.

4 Stir in mushrooms and sun-dried tomatoes. Cover; cook on Low heat setting 20 to 30 minutes longer or until sun-dried tomatoes are tender. Serve beef mixture over noodles; sprinkle with parsley.

1 Serving: Calories 270 (Calories from Fat 140); Total Fat 15g (Saturated Fat 6g); Cholesterol 70mg; Sodium 430mg; Total Carbohydrate 9g (Dietary Fiber 2g); Protein 25g

To save time, you may want to use beef stew meat instead of cutting the beef roast into pieces. If you prefer, you can use beef broth instead of the wine.

Beef and Potato Stew

Prep Time: 20 min ▪ Start to Finish: 8 hr 35 min ▪ 6 Servings

1 cup sun-dried tomatoes (not in oil)
1½ lb beef stew meat
12 small new potatoes (1½ lb), cut in half
1 medium onion, cut into 8 wedges
1½ cups ready-to-eat baby-cut carrots
1 can (14 oz) beef broth
1½ teaspoons seasoned salt
1 dried bay leaf
½ cup water
¼ cup all-purpose flour

1 Cover dried tomatoes with boiling water. Let stand 10 minutes; drain. Coarsely chop tomatoes.

2 In 3½- to 4-quart slow cooker, mix tomatoes and remaining ingredients except water and flour.

3 Cover and cook on Low heat setting 8 to 9 hours.

4 Mix water and flour; gradually stir into stew. Increase heat setting to High. Cover and cook 10 to 15 minutes or until slightly thickened. Remove bay leaf.

1 Serving: Calories 350 (Calories from Fat 125); Total Fat 14g (Saturated Fat 5g); Cholesterol 70mg; Sodium 900mg; Total Carbohydrate 34g (Dietary Fiber 4g); Protein 28g

Serve a loaf of crusty French bread with this stew so everyone can soak up all of the rich, flavorful gravy in the bottom of the bowl.

Down-South Pork Stew

Prep Time: 20 min ▪ Start to Finish: 6 hr 20 min ▪ 6 Servings

1½ lb boneless pork shoulder
¼ cup all-purpose flour
½ teaspoon peppered seasoned salt
1 tablespoon vegetable oil
2 medium dark-orange sweet potatoes, peeled, cut into ¾-inch cubes (3 cups)
1 cup frozen whole kernel corn (from 1-lb bag), thawed
1 can (15 to 16 oz) black-eyed peas, rinsed, drained
1 can (14 oz) roasted garlic-seasoned chicken broth
2 tablespoons Worcestershire sauce
½ teaspoon dried thyme leaves
⅛ teaspoon ground red pepper (cayenne)

1 Cut pork into ¾-inch cubes. In large bowl, toss pork, flour and peppered seasoned salt. In 12-inch nonstick skillet, heat oil over medium-high heat. Cook pork in oil 8 to 10 minutes, stirring occasionally, until brown.

2 In 3- to 4-quart slow cooker, mix pork and remaining ingredients.

3 Cover and cook on Low heat setting 6 to 7 hours.

1 Serving: Calories 405 (Calories from Fat 155); Total Fat 17g (Saturated Fat 5g); Cholesterol 75mg; Sodium 660mg; Total Carbohydrate 37g (Dietary Fiber 7g); Protein 33g

When time is tight, you can skip the step of browning the meat (and omit the oil).

Asian Pork Stew

Prep Time: 25 min ▪ Start to Finish: 7 hr 25 min ▪ 8 Servings

2 lb boneless country-style pork ribs,
    cut into 2-inch pieces
3 medium carrots, cut into 1-inch slices
2 medium onions, cut into 1-inch wedges
1 package (8 oz) fresh whole
    mushrooms, cut in half if large
1 can (8 oz) whole water chestnuts,
    drained
1 can (8 oz) bamboo shoots, drained
¾ cup hoisin sauce

⅓ cup reduced-sodium soy sauce
4 large cloves garlic, finely chopped
1 tablespoon finely chopped gingerroot
4 cups water
2 cups uncooked long-grain white rice
2 tablespoons cornstarch
3 tablespoons water
⅓ cup lightly packed coarsely
    chopped cilantro

1 Spray 5- to 6-quart slow cooker with cooking spray. In cooker, layer pork, carrots, onions, mushrooms, water chestnuts and bamboo shoots. In small bowl, stir together ½ cup of the hoisin sauce, the soy sauce, garlic and gingerroot; pour into slow cooker.

2 Cover; cook on Low heat setting 7 to 9 hours.

3 During last hour of cooking, in 3-quart saucepan, heat 4 cups water and the rice to boiling over high heat. Reduce heat to low. Cover; simmer 15 to 20 minutes or until rice is tender and water is absorbed.

4 Gently remove pork and vegetables with slotted spoon to large bowl; cover to keep warm. Skim any fat from liquid in cooker. Pour liquid into 1-quart saucepan. Stir remaining ¼ cup hoisin sauce into liquid; heat to boiling. In small bowl, mix cornstarch and 3 tablespoons water; stir into liquid. Cook, stirring constantly, until thickened; pour over pork mixture and gently stir.

5 Sprinkle cilantro over stew. Serve over rice.

1 Serving: Calories 510 (Calories from Fat 130); Total Fat 15g (Saturated Fat 5g); Cholesterol 70mg; Sodium 810mg; Total Carbohydrate 63g (Dietary Fiber 3g); Protein 30g

Hearty Pork Stew

Prep Time: 35 min ▮ Start to Finish: 7 hr 20 min ▮ 6 Servings

1 tablespoon vegetable oil

1½ lb boneless pork loin roast, cut into 1-inch cubes

3 medium carrots, cut into ¼-inch slices (1½ cups)

1 medium onion, chopped (½ cup)

2 cups ½-inch cubes peeled parsnips

1½ cups 1-inch cubes peeled butternut squash

4 cups chicken broth

1 tablespoon chopped fresh or 1 teaspoon dried sage leaves

2 teaspoons chopped fresh or ¾ teaspoon dried thyme leaves

½ teaspoon salt

½ teaspoon pepper

3 tablespoons all-purpose flour

3 tablespoons butter or margarine, softened

1 In 10-inch skillet, heat oil over medium-high heat. Cook pork in oil 6 to 8 minutes, stirring occasionally, until browned on all sides.

2 In 3-quart slow cooker, mix pork and remaining ingredients except flour and butter.

3 Cover and cook on Low heat setting 6 to 7 hours.

4 Mix flour and butter; gradually stir into stew until blended. Increase heat setting to High. Cover and cook 30 to 45 minutes, stirring occasionally, until thickened.

1 Serving: Calories 365 (Calories from Fat 160); Total Fat 18g (Saturated Fat 7g); Cholesterol 90mg; Sodium 980mg; Total Carbohydrate 21g (Dietary Fiber 4g); Protein 30g

Sage and thyme help give this cozy stew its autumn flair. For extra embellishment, add a sprig of fresh thyme or some chopped fresh sage leaves to each serving.

Chicken Stew

Prep Time: 10 min ▌ Start to Finish: 8 hr 10 min ▌ 6 Servings

3 medium potatoes (about 1 lb), cut into 1½-inch cubes
2 cups ready-to-eat baby-cut carrots
1 package (8 oz) fresh whole mushrooms, each cut in half
2 packages (20 oz each) boneless skinless chicken thighs
½ teaspoon salt
1 teaspoon dried chopped onion
¼ teaspoon garlic powder
1½ jars (12 oz each) chicken gravy (about 2¼ cups)
1 tablespoon tomato paste
½ cup dry white wine or water
2 tablespoons chopped fresh parsley, if desired

1 Spray 4- to 5-quart slow cooker with cooking spray. In cooker, toss potatoes, carrots and mushrooms. Arrange chicken on vegetable mixture. Sprinkle salt, onion and garlic powder over chicken. Stir together gravy and tomato paste. Pour gravy mixture and wine over all.

2 Cover; cook on Low heat setting 8 to 10 hours. Sprinkle servings with parsley.

1 Serving: Calories 460 (Calories from Fat 180); Total Fat 20g (Saturated Fat 6g); Cholesterol 120mg; Sodium 870mg; Total Carbohydrate 24g (Dietary Fiber 4g); Protein 44g

A sprinkling of fresh parsley can add spark to any slow-cooked recipe.

African Groundnut Stew with Chicken

Prep Time: 20 min ▪ Start to Finish: 8 hr 20 min ▪ 8 Servings

6 boneless skinless chicken thighs (about 1 lb)
3 boneless skinless chicken breasts (about ¾ lb)
1 medium onion, chopped (1 cup)
¾ cup peanut butter
1 can (28 oz) diced tomatoes, undrained
1 can (14 oz) chicken broth
2 tablespoons grated gingerroot
2 tablespoons tomato paste
2 teaspoons curry powder
1 teaspoon crushed red pepper flakes
½ teaspoon salt
1½ lb sweet potatoes (3 medium), peeled, cubed (about 4 cups)
1 lb small red potatoes (about 12), cut into eighths (about 2½ cups)

1 Spray 5- to 6-quart slow cooker with cooking spray. In cooker, layer all ingredients, spooning peanut butter in dollops.

2 Cover; cook on Low heat setting 8 to 10 hours. Break up chicken before serving.

1 Serving: Calories 420 (Calories from Fat 170); Total Fat 19g (Saturated Fat 5g); Cholesterol 60mg; Sodium 710mg; Total Carbohydrate 32g (Dietary Fiber 6g); Protein 31g

Tomato paste is available in tubes and cans. Look for it in the supermarket next to the canned tomato products.

Mediterranean Chicken Stew

Prep Time: 10 min ▪ Start to Finish: 5 hr 20 min ▪ 5 Servings

2 teaspoons olive or vegetable oil
2 lb boneless skinless chicken thighs
1 teaspoon garlic salt
¼ teaspoon pepper
2 teaspoons dried oregano leaves
2 cans (14.5 oz each) diced tomatoes with garlic and onion, undrained
1 can (14 oz) quartered artichoke hearts, drained
1 package (10 oz) couscous (1½ cups)
1 can (6 oz) pitted medium ripe olives, drained

1 In 12-inch skillet, heat oil over medium-high heat. Sprinkle chicken with garlic salt, pepper and oregano. Cook chicken in oil 8 minutes, turning once, until brown on both sides; drain. Place chicken, tomatoes and artichokes in 4- to 4½-quart slow cooker.

2 Cover and cook on Low heat setting 5 to 6 hours.

3 Cook couscous as directed on package. Stir olives into stew. To serve, spoon stew over couscous.

1 Serving: Calories 605 (Calories from Fat 190); Total Fat 21g (Saturated Fat 5g); Cholesterol 115mg; Sodium 1040mg; Total Carbohydrate 64g (Dietary Fiber 10g); Protein 50g

For a medley of Mediterranean flavors, serve this stew with a fresh spinach salad topped with crumbled feta cheese and sliced fresh figs. Sesame or poppy seed–topped bread makes a great accompaniment.

Helpful Nutrition and Cooking Information

Recommended intake for a daily diet of 2,000 calories as set by the Food and Drug Administration

Total Fat	Less than 65g
Saturated Fat	Less than 20g
Cholesterol	Less than 300mg
Sodium	Less than 2,400mg
Total Carbohydrate	300g
Dietary Fiber	25g

Calculating Nutrition Information

- The first ingredient is used wherever a choice is given (such as ⅓ cup sour cream or plain yogurt).

- The first ingredient amount is used wherever a range is given (such as 2 to 3 teaspoons).

- The first serving number was used wherever a range is given (such as 4 to 6 servings).

- "If desired" ingredients and recipe variations were not included (such as sprinkle with brown sugar, if desired).

- Only the amount of a marinade or frying oil that is absorbed by the food during preparation was calculated.

Ingredients Used in Recipe Testing and Nutrition Calculations

The following ingredients, based on most commonly purchased ingredients, are used unless indicated otherwise:

- Large eggs, 2% milk, 80%-lean ground beef, canned chicken broth and vegetable oil spread containing at least 65% fat when margarine is used.

- Solid vegetable shortening (not butter, margarine, or nonstick cooking spray) is used to grease pans.

Equipment Used in Recipe Testing

- Cookware and bakeware without nonstick coatings were used, unless otherwise indicated.

- No dark-colored, black or insulated bakeware was used.

- When a pan is specified, a metal pan was used; a baking dish or pie plate means ovenproof glass was used.

- An electric hand mixer was used for mixing when mixer speeds are specified.

Metric Conversion Guide

VOLUME

U.S. Units	Canadian Metric	Australian Metric
¼ teaspoon	1 mL	1 ml
½ teaspoon	2 mL	2 ml
1 teaspoon	5 mL	5 ml
1 tablespoon	15 mL	20 ml
¼ cup	50 mL	60 ml
⅓ cup	75 mL	80 ml
½ cup	125 mL	125 ml
⅔ cup	150 mL	170 ml
¾ cup	175 mL	190 ml
1 cup	250 mL	250 ml
1 quart	1 liter	1 liter
1 ½ quarts	1.5 liters	1.5 liters
2 quarts	2 liters	2 liters
2 ½ quarts	2.5 liters	2.5 liters
3 quarts	3 liters	3 liters
4 quarts	4 liters	4 liters

WEIGHT

U.S. Units	Canadian Metric	Australian Metric
1 ounce	30 grams	30 grams
2 ounces	55 grams	60 grams
3 ounces	85 grams	90 grams
4 ounces (¼ pound)	115 grams	125 grams
8 ounces (½ pound)	225 grams	225 grams
16 ounces (1 pound)	455 grams	500 grams
1 pound	455 grams	½ kilogram

MEASUREMENTS

Inches	Centimeters
1	2.5
2	5.0
3	7.5
4	10.0
5	12.5
6	15.0
7	17.5
8	20.5
9	23.0
10	25.5
11	28.0
12	30.5
13	33.0

TEMPERATURES

Fahrenheit	Celsius
32°	0°
212°	100°
250°	120°
275°	140°
300°	150°
325°	160°
350°	180°
375°	190°
400°	200°
425°	220°
450°	230°
475°	240°
500°	260°

NOTE: The recipes in this cookbook have not been developed or tested using metric measures. When converting recipes to metric, some variations in quality may be noted.

Index

Page numbers in italics indicate illustrations.

Whatever's on the menu, make it easy with *Betty Crocker*

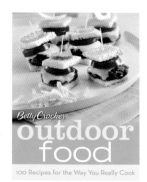

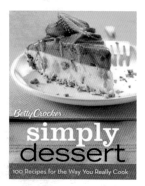